Facing the Mirror

Finding a *Self* to Live With

Daphne Delay

www.mirrorministries.org

Published by Mirror Ministries, Inc.
PO Box 1418
Seminole TX 79360

Page design by Daphne Delay.

Cover/Author Photo: Veronica Bernal | *www.chiaro-perfecto.com*

Printed in the United States of America

Delay, Daphne
    Facing the Mirror: Finding a Self to Live With.

    ISBN 978-0-9745379-1-7
    1. Spiritual growth. 2. Christian living.

To my husband Tod, who always says, "I don't have to read it... I lived it!"—Thank you for being such a godly man. I love how you make me laugh (and sometimes roll my eyes). And I am very grateful for the life God has created for me with you. To my children, Emily, Christopher, Benjamin, and the sweet addition of my daughter-in-law Tya. Each of you mean so very much to me. You have taught me many things and I believe I'm a better person because of your love and influence. To my dear friends, Karen and Michel, who never stopped encouraging me to spread this message in written form. Your support has been an anchor.

And to the beautiful people who haven't known about, or fully understood, the righteousness God has established for us all.

Table of Contents

Introduction

God Wants You to Know

In 1999, I was standing at the front of a stage in Ruidoso, New Mexico, after fearfully sharing my testimony with over 100 women. The Holy Spirit had prodded me before breakfast to spread the word for everyone to bring a mirror with them to the conference room. After speaking, I challenged the ladies to look in their mirrors and tell the girl looking back that they loved her and forgave her. I had never given these instructions to such a large group before, and wasn't sure what to expect. But within minutes, the place began erupting with praise as one by one, women were being healed and set free from the lies of the enemy.

In that moment, as I stood in awe of what God was doing with the simple message of righteousness, the Holy Spirit whispered to me, *"Write it down and I'll put it in the hands of people you'll never meet."*

I wish I could tell you I obeyed immediately, but I didn't. My first thought was, Who would buy a book from a girl in Seminole? Followed by, I wouldn't know what to write.

For the next eighteen months, I ran from God's instruction.

My mom and I attended many women's conferences together and each time I was near a speaker's book table, my stomach would get butterflies and I'd have to go back to my seat.

On a separate occasion, while at a pastor's conference with my husband, I visited the campus bookstore. The same butterflies flittered inside but I pushed them away trying to make excuses for why I wasn't the right candidate for the job. The next speaker gave a powerful testimony of the miraculous ways in which God answers prayer and uses people. At the end of his message, he had us stand to our feet and give God thanks for what He was doing in our lives.

As I lifted my heart and hands to Heaven and sincerely thanked God for salvation and the work He was doing in our church, He said to me, *"If you won't do it, I'll find someone who will."*

My heart was so convicted. I knew what He was referring to. I loved Jesus and although I wasn't sure how He was going to use me, I repented for my selfishness and said yes.

Another eighteen months passed before I completed my assignment and published, <u>Take a Closer Look</u>, in 2003. And to my amazement, once I obeyed and began to write,

God flooded my understanding with new revelation of His righteousness. Since then, I have been privileged to see God dramatically change lives through this message.

As I continued to speak, teach, and write on this topic—helping others discover the same truths I'd found—the Lord began prompting me to write what I thought would be an expanded version of my first book. I certainly had more stories, testimonies, and scripture to add, so I readily said yes this time. But in the end, it was an entirely new book altogether. And I believe, as with all good things from God, it was meant for such a time as this.

Or should I say, *it was meant for such a one as you!*

God wants you to know how He sees you—versus how you've always seen yourself.

And I have to add, writing this book was easy because I know God wants to use you just as He's used me. His righteousness has a purpose. And your understanding of it will open amazing doors!

Forever in His debt,

Daphne

Chapter One

Through the Fire and Past the Mirror

*Love yourself, for if you don't
how can you expect anybody else to love you?*
-Author Unknown

What are people looking for? Really?

It seems there is something in every person's inner core—regardless of that person's background—that cries out for a standard, a set of guidelines they can believe in, adhere to, and find fulfillment through.

It's what helps them stay focused and on the right course. It's what guides them back if they get lost. It's like the voice on our GPS that won't stop saying, "Turn around. Turn around. Turn around..." when we've missed the mark and find ourselves on a path we didn't intend to travel.

But what if you don't have that guidance system? Or

what if it wasn't developed in you at an early age?

The Summer of 2010

I didn't understand why the officer said what he did, but I acknowledged it nonetheless. "Ma'am, your son is not dead."

This was the phone call parents dread. Our nineteen-year-old son, Benjamin, had left earlier that day to make the nine-hour drive back to Tulsa where he was attending Bible School. He had been with us for Father's Day after a month-long trip to Alaska to help his best friends move their parents. The three boys had invited another young man to move to Tulsa after graduating high school to live with them and get his feet wet in independence.

Benjamin agreed to stay behind one day to help Cameron load his truck, and then the two would travel together. Benjamin had made this trip many times and nothing seemed out of the ordinary as they pulled out laden with all of Cameron's belongings tied down and loaded to the gill in his old pickup.

Seven hours later, my cell phone rang. "Mrs. Delay, this is

Officer Smith with the Oklahoma State Highway Patrol. Your son is not dead..." When the officer came to the hospital later to check on us, I finally understood why he worded his statement the way he did. In all his years in the highway patrol, he had never found survivors in an accident as horrific as the one Benjamin and Cameron experienced.

It's not clear if the boys dozed off, which seemed unlikely in the middle of the day, or if the gravel on the side of the road caused their truck to pull to the left. But either way, in a fraction of a second, the driver-side door grazed a guardrail. At the normal highway speed of seventy miles an hour, it only took another fraction of a second for the guardrail to scrape the side of the pickup, pop the gas tank behind the driver-side door, catch the rim of the back tire, and flip them up in mid-air... *igniting the truck on fire like a matchbox.*

The driver of a semi-truck behind the boys said he'd never seen anything like it. The pickup flipped only one and a half times, landing on it's top facing the opposite direction in the ditch on the other side of the road, engulfed in flames.

Cameron's elbow had smashed the driver-side window, giving him a way out. As he ran around to Benjamin's side to open his door, the flames were already too hot to reach him. Benjamin was in the truck locked upside-down in his seatbelt. Running back around to the broken window, Cameron found Benjamin pulling himself out, and helped him the rest of the way. Not knowing if the truck would explode, the two boys attempted to run from the increasing flames, but Benjamin collapsed 10 feet from the pickup and had to be carried to safety.

Lying in the hot sun, on the side of the highway awaiting emergency crews, it became apparent the boys were injured. Strangers who had stopped to help shielded them with blankets and their own shadows to block the blistering sun. We wouldn't know the extent of their injuries until later that evening, but for sure, Cameron was bleeding and Benjamin's exposed feet, legs, arms, and face were burned.

A Defining Moment

Benjamin had always been a happy, witty child. In second grade, my husband was asked to be the Senior

Pastor at a church in the small, West Texas town of Seminole. Although we moved midyear, it didn't take long for Benjamin to make friends at the church and on his summer baseball team.

There were six years between our two boys, and by Benjamin's ninth birthday, a little sister had joined our family. Over the next few months, and into the start of another school year, Benjamin began to withdraw and became uncharacteristically quiet. I suspected it had a little to do with the attention our two young toddlers received from everyone. They looked like their daddy with olive skin, and as with most children, they were just "cute" at that age.

Benjamin favored my side of the family with beautiful reddish-auburn hair and freckles. He was a handsome young man, but I recognized in him something I had wrestled with myself as a young girl—I didn't like looking different.

One night as I tucked him in bed, I questioned him about his unusual behavior. He was young and didn't know how to answer me, so I got him out of bed and stood him before the mirror over his desk. "What do you think about that boy?" I said. With a quick glance in the mirror and then eyes closed, he said, "I hate him. He's ugly."

No Matter Who You Are

Insecurity is an evil. It doesn't matter if you're young or old, male or female, American or European. Every human being has to come face-to-face with insecurity at some point in time. With the best of intentions, our friends and family can tell us how wonderful and loved we are, but unless we believe it for ourselves, insecurity has the ability to squelch dreams, mask truth, and redefine destinies. *"For as he thinks in his heart, so is he" (Proverbs 23:7a).*

God has created every person unique with individual gifts, talents, and callings. But with the world and media constantly blasting their idea of perfection on each new generation, it's hard to find your true self in the mix. From kids on the playground to executives in a boardroom, insecurities can arise from comparisons and a lack of inner confidence—and that's if you are close to perfect by the world's standards.

So what about the person who was abused or neglected as a child? How do the injured, the maimed, the rejected, and the self-inflicted find confidence in who they are in a world that barely lets the "beautiful and perfect" person survive?

Look in the Mirror

"Benjamin, that boy is not ugly. Look at him. Look in his eyes."

> *Life is a mirror and will reflect back to the thinker what he thinks into it.*
> -Earnest Holmes

God had placed me in front of my mirror many years prior, and now the lesson that had redefined who I was would be the very lesson that would protect my son's destiny.

Benjamin looked into the mirror again and as he did, I said, "That little boy was created by God and is loved by Him and many others. He needs to know that you love him too. Look into his eyes Benjamin. He's scared because he knows you don't love him. But God has a plan for that boy."

The Bible says, *"Don't copy the behavior and customs of*

this world, but let God transform you into a new person by changing the way you think" (Romans 12:2).[1]

Benjamin acknowledged what I said without saying a word but accepted a hug and a kiss on the forehead as I tucked him back into bed that night.

Over the next few weeks, I prayed and our vibrant young son blossomed again as if nothing had ever happened. He continued through school, emerging as a leader in both his youth group and among his peers. Benjamin graduated with top honors and was a talented drummer with dreams of "saving the world" with his music and sheer enthusiasm. He chose to attend Rhema Bible Training Center[2] after high school following in his dad's footsteps (Benjamin had been just five years old when his dad graduated from Rhema).

Now ten years after the defining moment in front of his mirror, Benjamin was lying on the side of the road with third degree burns on over one-third of his body.

Destinies Compete

As I stood by his bed in ICU, he was unrecognizable.

Moments earlier, the nurse had shown us a colored diagram of the percent of his burns. She said, "His age will help him. We add his age to his percent of severe burns to determine his mortality rate." I thought, Did I hear her right... mortality rate? At my son's side, I could barely process this information.

I had stood by the bedside of many critical patients before. As pastors, my husband and I have been called in to pray with and encourage the faith of families in desperate situations. We have reminded loved ones of God's faithfulness to His Word and comforted families and individuals with hope and peace despite all odds. Many situations turned into triumphant testimonies, while some left us with nagging thoughts of "Why God?" And with no sure answer, in our pastoral role we would pray for *"peace that passes understanding"* [3] for all involved.

But this time, I wasn't the pastor—I was the parent. More specifically, I was the mother. If I could believe for others and not for myself, doesn't that make God's Word a lie? I couldn't allow my faith to change because it was now my son in the bed, no matter what it looked like.

I wouldn't allow myself to entertain thoughts of death. Instead, my biggest fear in that moment was the nagging concern of what Benjamin would look like when he healed, and how would he handle it?

So there is only one of two things a parent can do in this situation: have faith in God or carry a burden of worry and fear. I could not do both. Thankfully, I had hidden God's Word in my heart (first for myself, and secondly for others); and it now brought great comfort to me. David was right when he said, *"Unless Your law had been my delight, I would then have perished in my affliction"* (Psalm 119:92).

We were told to expect Benjamin to be hospitalized for some time. He was on a ventilator to help repair the damage to his lungs and throat after breathing in the fire, and skin graft surgeries were a certainty. His burns covered multiple joint areas, which meant therapy and possible loss of mobility. As a talented drummer with a great future, this news was almost unacceptable— although we couldn't downplay the fact that he was alive and we'd face tomorrow together whatever it may be.

Each night, my husband and I would be forced to leave ICU and the comfort we found in being by our son's bedside looking for any and all signs of improvement. As human as we were, we would look at each other and make the same statement night after night: "Tell me he's going to be okay."

Despite a swirl of emotions, I was reminded of Abraham's faith and how *"...contrary to hope, in hope [he] believed" (Romans 4:18).* Now was my moment of truth. As any mother would, I cried as I looked at my broken child. Yet in that moment, I made a decision: I will not cry for tomorrow... for God's Word is true and His faithfulness shall be my strength.

The next day, I wrote in my journal:

> I am fully convinced of God's Word. We will have victory in the midst of this trial. I have not lost heart because I am confident I will see the goodness of the Lord in the land of the living (Psalm 27:13). Just as Abraham chose not to rely only on natural hope (what you can do based on what others are saying), but instead chose to believe according to spiritual hope (what GOD can DO based on what HE HAS SAID) — I have chosen the same.

Seven weeks and six surgeries later, Benjamin was released from the hospital. He had endured a tracheotomy and many painful skin grafts. Because he had taken his shoes off in the pickup, his burns completely wrapped his right foot and lower leg to the knee. The flames on the passenger-side door had also engulfed his right hand, arm, and face. The left side of his body had severe second-degree burns, but none that needed grafting.

When we left the hospital, Benjamin's 6'4" frame carried only 132 pounds—twenty pounds lighter than before the accident. Most of his exposed skin was deep red and purplish in color, clinging to the fresh grafts. But his handsome red hair and confident wit soon took all onlookers past the scars.

And without a doubt, Benjamin's future—tough as it would be—was secure because he had learned at an early age about righteousness and who he was in God's eyes. He had discovered and developed a faith he could live by, a purpose he could live for, *and a self he could live with*—long before he found himself on a path he didn't intend to travel.

Chapter Two

"You be (like) Jesus"

The art of pleasing is the art of deception.
-Luc de Clapiers

The Lord God said, *"Let us make man in Our image, according to our likeness."* [1] So God created man and woman in His own image and placed them in a beautiful garden. But the serpent was more cunning than any other beast which the Lord had made, and he tempted the woman to disobey God therefore introducing sin. Then the eyes of both the man and the woman were opened and they knew they were naked, so they sewed fig leaves together and made themselves clothing. When God discovered what they had done, He sacrificed one of the animals to make lasting clothes of skin for them, but as He presented the new clothing to the man and the woman, they said, "No Lord, we're not worthy—we'll keep our fig leaves." And they rejected that which the Lord God had done for them.

OK, not an entirely true story from the Bible... *but true in real life nonetheless.*

Many Christians, although they've accepted Jesus as their Savior, are wearing layers of imaginary fig leaves because they don't feel worthy of His sacrifice. Like Adam and Eve, they began by covering their inadequacies with a small leaf at first, but quickly discovered it didn't hide their sins from God, so they moved on to bigger leaves. But when their feelings of unworthiness were still exposed, it seemed only natural to dress themselves in something tougher—like the bark of a tree—expecting it to be more durable, protective, and harder to see through.

But the truth is, we don't need fig leaves, bark, or any other mask or covering to establish our self-worth. As Christians, our *"...life is HIDDEN with Christ in God" (Colossians 3:3).* Jesus is our covering. It doesn't matter who you are— if you struggle with regrets, failures, or low self-esteem, you are actually struggling with understanding (and receiving) the most beautiful gift God has ever given to man.

Adam and Eve didn't really reject what God had done for them, but we do know they were ashamed. Because of their actions, they were embarrassed, humiliated, and most likely, in a state of disgrace as they put on the clothing God provided for them.

And centuries later, you and I aren't much different.

Daphne didn't like Daphne

I remember hearing a story about a mother and her two young boys who were in the kitchen one morning preparing breakfast. As this mother poured the pancake batter, her sons began arguing over who was going to get the first pancake. Seeing an opportunity to teach them a lesson, she said, "You know Jesus would let His brother have the first pancake." The boys immediately stopped arguing. Then, after a short pause, the older brother looked at the younger and said, "Okay, you be Jesus."

Cute story, but all too real for me... Not because I had young boys who argued over pancakes (which I did), but because my entire life had been about trying to measure up to the expectations of others (you know, the "You be

16

Jesus" part).

When I was much younger, my goal was to be popular—
something I didn't feel came easy for me. In junior high, I
ran for class president, won, and held the position
through my senior year. And although I appeared to
have some status among my peers, I later realized the

> *The greatest deception men suffer is from their own opinions.*
>
> -Leonardo da Vinci

"leader" in me was really just a
follower. In other words,
whatever pleased others is what
I did. My heart had deep-rooted
insecurities.

As a young person, when I looked in the mirror I didn't
see the same beauty I admired in all my friends.
Psychologists would suggest it was because I didn't have
a regular father figure in my life to tell me I was
something special or beautiful. They may or may not be
right, but I felt loved and accepted by my family. In fact,
although my parents had divorced and remarried a
couple of times, I don't remember ever feeling rejected
by either of them. My granddad on my mother's side was
always around and very supportive, and both my real
dad and stepdad showed me great love.

So I would have to disagree with the psychologists. My problem was *Daphne didn't like Daphne*, and my eyes deceived me often. When I didn't see the same beauty in my mirror as the magazines, television, or peer pressure portrayed, I fell into the traps of alcohol, drugs, and promiscuity, looking for acceptance.

But these empty acts only increased the disapproval that stared me down each time I stood before my pitiful reflection.

"You be (like) Jesus"

Through a series of events and very bad choices, which landed me at the bottom of the bottom with nowhere to look but up, I found salvation at the age of 21. At first, I was elated. The love and peace I felt in the sanctuary of God's presence was unlike anything I had ever known before. But little by little, what I believed about myself *before* salvation soon overrode any and everything I was being told about Jesus and His love for me now.

My deceived heart only heard, "You be (like) Jesus,"— which was something I definitely could not do.

I had well-kept secrets, and although I'd done a good job

of hiding them from those around me, deep down I knew God was well aware of my past. So I believed if the goal was to be like Jesus, I had already blown that a million times over and nothing could change or reverse it.

Ironically, the same year I was saved, I met a young Christian man at the church I was attending, fell in love, became pregnant, and got married. (Yes, in that order.) I already wrestled with condemnation (what the dictionary would define as a self-pronounced sentence of guilt), and I now had one more thing to pile on my heap of disgrace:

I couldn't even be a good Christian, much less be like Jesus.

But despite my struggles, God's Word became my lifeline to eternity. I clung to every promise of heaven hoping God would receive me *someday*. My goal was to survive until I would finally and forever be free from the condemnation that tainted everything about me.

Can you relate?

You don't have to be a young, white woman, in middle-class America to struggle with these same issues. Guilt, regrets, insecurities, and condemnation are all weapons of Satan to destroy God's people (preferably before they come to Christ to keep them lost; but definitely after, to keep them from sharing their faith with others).

Satan's best-laid plan has always been for us to destroy ourselves first.

At any stage of life, Satan loves using the weaknesses of our flesh as a weapon against us; much like the bully who grabs our wrist, swinging it toward our face, yelling, "Quit hitting yourself! Quit hitting yourself!" Satan targets our insecurities and then laughs at our self-destruction. The Bible says we fall into his snare and are *"taken captive by him to do his will" (2 Timothy 2:26).*

By all appearances, I looked as though I had it all together after salvation. I wore my mask well, but my mirror remained an enemy. Every time I looked into it, I inevitably found something wrong. My husband and family assured me of their love, but I struggled receiving it because I didn't love myself. Don't get me wrong, I disliked the torture I felt on the inside, but not knowing how to end it, I simply prayed silent prayers for God's deliverance.

In my mind, an imaginary glass box imprisoned me. I could see through the top, bottom, and sides, peering out at all the perfect people in the world—yet it caged me nonetheless. As I viewed my world and others through these false walls, I perceived that, unlike myself, everyone around me must have lived lives worthy of God's approval. There were times when I would forget or become numb to my feelings for a moment and then without notice—Bang! —I would hit the top of that see-through box.

Inevitably something would "put me back in my place," and remind me of my guilt, shame, and regret for my sins—all of which confined and limited my freedom.

In Romans 7:24, the Apostle Paul said, *"O wretched man that I am! Who will deliver me from this body of death?"* I could definitely relate to this statement. But he went on to say, *"I thank God—through Jesus Christ our Lord!"* And it was this part of his testimony I didn't understand. Was he talking about heaven? Or something else?

It didn't take long for God to answer my questions. And what happened next in my life changed everything...

The Mirror Doesn't Lie

It was like any other morning, except for one small detail. As I stood in front of my bathroom mirror preparing for the day, I heard a voice. I'm not sure if you would have heard it if you were with me that morning, but it was very clear to me. And although I was still far from being a mature Christian at the time, I knew it was God.

He said, *"Look closer."*

As I looked into the mirror at my reflection, I expected to find something wrong (again). Was my hair out of place? Were my freckles uncovered? Is this blouse too tight?

But God said, *"No. Look close. Look deep into your eyes."*

As I moved closer to the mirror and looked into my own eyes, I looked at another person. The eyes in the mirror reflected a girl who knew my secret thoughts, fears, disappointments, hopes, and dreams. For years I had attempted to hide her because she was the one guilty of all my mistakes. I had carefully hidden her away while I focused on the exterior part of myself that others saw.

Yet as I stood there within an inch of the mirror, looking at nothing but those eyes—eyes reflecting great sorrow, God said, *"Now tell her you love her and you forgive her."*

Standing face to face with my torturer, I was so surprised at who had held me captive all these years. I don't recall believing God was my torturer, but I did believe He was the one who held the key to my glass box (my imaginary prison). Trusting He knew best, I had accepted the imprisonment as an appropriate punishment for my failures. I could see God on the outside. I could see everyone and I envied them. "Be grateful," I would tell myself. "God has allowed you to come this far; don't ask for more," and I never did.

Yet there I stood, facing my mirror, with the answer to my silent prayer. The key had always been in my hand. The lock was inside.

Whereas I had believed my sins were too great for God to pardon, I now had to face the realization it wasn't God who was withholding forgiveness. The make-believe prison was my own doing—Daphne couldn't forgive Daphne.

In One Sentence

Glued to the blue eyes looking back at me, I had flashbacks of horror stories I had heard about abused children locked in closets. The eyes in my mirror belonged to someone just like that—locked away, unloved, and unforgiven. And like a child who didn't know what they've done to deserve such treatment, the eyes in my mirror reflected fear, confusion, pain and rejection.

Unable to look away, I cried a steady stream of tears for almost an hour as I tried to unlock my imaginary glass box and accept the truth.

"Tell her you love her and you forgive her."

In one sentence God showed me that although I had accepted His Son as my Savior and received His promise for eternal life in heaven, I had never accepted His forgiveness for my sins. I didn't feel worthy of such forgiveness. Surely He knew all I had done? Didn't He know how many times I had failed? How could He forgive me? This kind of love and forgiveness was beyond my comprehension.

I had lived in a vacuum of comparison for so long, striving for the goal of perfection and approval.

"Tell her you love her and you forgive her."

I held the key.

In front of my mirror, God revealed His truth: *"If any person be in Christ Jesus, they are a new creation; the old has passed away, behold, all things have become new" (2 Corinthians 5:17).* At salvation, I knew my heart was drastically changed. Yet I was struggling between the old sinful person I was so ashamed of and the new person who was forgiven. But contrary to my emotions and self-judgments, I had to free that hurting child in my mirror. So with forced effort and through sobbing tears, I looked close into my own eyes and finally said those words: I love you and I forgive you.

In His wisdom, the Lord knew my guilt and shame were deep-rooted. Simply saying the words "I love you and I forgive you" only scratched the surface. My problem had to be uprooted with sincerity. In other words, I had to mean what I said.

When I was a child, I remember having to pull weeds as part of my chores. Some weeds could be pulled up easily because they had very little roots. Others took a lot of pull and effort because they had deep roots. I soon learned weeds with roots left in the ground only grow back. That lesson served me well in front of my mirror... I don't know if another hour passed, but after more effort and many more tears, I yanked up the roots of condemnation and said again—and more sincerely—*"I love you and I forgive you."*

Finally, the door of my glass box swung open. Like the unloved child released from their dark closet, the girl in my mirror was freed from unforgiveness.

Forever Changed

Our eyes serve as windows to our soul, the real us. We look into mirrors at our reflection all the time, but we only see our exterior. Yet how we view ourselves will have the greatest impact on our life than any other thing. Whereas we tend to look at the outside, God is able to look straight into our heart—into who we truly are. *"As in water, face reflects face, so a man's heart reveals the* man" *(Proverbs 27:19).*

I had personally been unable to see how my own insecurities, feelings of low self-worth, fears, failures, disappointments, and attempts to be someone I thought everyone wanted me to be, created the walls of my imaginary prison—my glass box. I built the walls out of a lack of knowledge of God's Word and His view of me. I didn't understand, much less comprehend, all I had received in Christ at salvation.

"Tell her you love her and you forgive her." The voice may not have been audible, but His words forever changed my life. Little did I know at the time however, God's written Word would soon seal what He began that day in front of my mirror.

Your Turn

My son Benjamin was able to pull through a horrific event in his life because he had learned at an early age that God doesn't see things the same way we do. And I was able to help him discover these truths because God so graciously revealed them to me despite my sinful past. The remainder of this book is designed to give you the same truths. And I fully believe you will experience the same results (no matter who you are or what you've endured) if you'll set your heart to believe it.

Chapter Three

Changing Clothes

One reason God created time was so there would be a place to bury the failures of the past.
-Author Unknown

In the Disney animated movie "Mulan," [1] there's a young girl who doesn't quite fit into her tradition-bound society. In attempts to bring honor to her family, she fails miserably. She tries to conform to handed-down traditions, but finds herself unable to fit into a mold made by others.

Embarrassed and ashamed, she hides from those who love her. While looking in a pool of water, she catches a glimpse of her own reflection and says to herself, "Who is this staring straight back at me? Why is my reflection someone I don't know? Somehow I cannot hide who I am... *though I've tried.* When will my reflection show who I am inside?"

Her father finally finds her and sensing her guilt and

condemnation, he lovingly sits beside her under a flowering tree and says, "What beautiful blossoms we have this year. But look, this one's late. But I bet when it blooms, it will be the most beautiful of all."

I was definitely a late bloomer. And I'm not just referring to physical development. Even after God's amazing revelation in front of my mirror, I was still slow to grasp all that I had received in Christ. But I couldn't deny (nor explain) the weight that had been lifted off my shoulders that day. And because we are creatures of habit, I would've eventually found myself right back where I started—guilty, insecure, and ashamed.

But the Holy Spirit began to regularly whisper a couple of scriptures to my heart. I'm sure I had heard these passages in a sermon at church, but I wasn't really familiar with them. However, each time I would make a mistake and sense an overwhelming feeling of guilt, the Holy Spirit would say, *"There's no condemnation for those who are in Christ Jesus."* And then He would say, *"You are the righteousness of God in Christ."*

Somehow I felt prompted to repeat these scriptures

aloud to myself, and as I did, the guilt would diminish. So for years, these confessions were my lifeline. It wasn't until 1999, while leading a Bible Study at my church, that I discovered the definition of the big-sounding word the Holy Spirit continually whispered to me.

In Beth Jones' workbook, <u>Getting a Grip on the Basics</u>,[2] she said, "Righteousness is right-standing with God and the ability to stand before Him without guilt or inferiority as if you had never sinned."

What?

By this time, I was a Pastor's wife and a lover of God's Word. I had confessed, *"I am the righteousness of God in Christ"* for years, but never fully knew what it meant! I had seen the "big-sounding word" in my Bible and had guessed it meant to be okay with God—*but to stand before Him without guilt...?* No way!

If I had known that was what I had been confessing, I would never have said it because it didn't describe how I viewed myself despite the love and forgiveness God had revealed to me in front of my mirror.

Conforming to the Mold

And this is why the story of Mulan is a good example of someone who doesn't understand who they truly are. The same is true of us as Christians when we lack understanding about our righteousness in Christ— meaning, what we've received through Jesus at salvation. If the reflection you see in the mirror is someone you don't know (or in some cases, don't like), that negative self-image will hinder your growth as a Christian and redefine your destiny.

Or, if you're a person who wrestles with regret, the result will be unnecessary condemnation. *(Remember the self-pronounced sentence of guilt?)* This then reflects in everything you do because everything runs off your inner image[3]—how you see yourself.

And for the most part, we're all guilty of trying to fit into a mold. Everywhere we turn, the media and traditions of men try to conform us. And we often give in to the pressure because we want to be accepted and please others. It's human nature. But when it comes to spiritual things, it really doesn't matter who we are (young, old,

educated, not educated, rich, poor, etc.)—each of us
wrestle with feeling inferior to others in small (or even
large) ways.

Some of us hide this well, while
others obviously pull to the
sidelines in fear and insecurity,
allowing their feelings of low

> *All men are not cast in the same mold.*
> -Author Unknown

self-worth to dominate their lives. God instructs us to be
humble, but He never intended for any of His children to
feel inferior or subordinate to others, much less,
unworthy of His approval.

Jesus died for all—and His righteousness was given for
all.

Much like Mulan, who eventually discovered the truth of
who she was and then lived it out despite all exterior
influences, I had to do the same. My son had to do the
same. In fact, our experiences were very different, yet
they had the potential of defining us either way.
Additionally, Benjamin had to face the fact that he was
going to carry the physical scars of his experience for the
rest of his life—*and be okay with that.*

He experienced a literal fire, whereas mine seemed more self-inflicted. But both of us had to face our mirror at some point or another. And in many cases, forgiveness is required.

The problem is that forgiveness is a funny thing. It's powerful enough to set you free and yet at the same time be the one thing you withhold the longest. That was my problem. I knew there had to be more to my relationship with God than I was experiencing—it just simply never dawned on me that my growth was suffering because of unforgiveness toward myself.

Punishment for the Crime

One thing I've learned is that Christians who struggle with forgiving themselves (for whatever reason) are tortured. Their lives are a vicious cycle of attempting to earn God's approval through their works, failing because the bar is set at perfection, feeling guilty for their failures and shortcomings, and then starting over again—with the same results day after day, and year after year.

This inward agony is much like an ancient practice of punishment for murder, which was once used in third-world countries.[4] If the accused were found guilty, the punishment for the murderer involved having the victim's dead body tied to his or her back. Then, as the corpse began to rot and decay, the murderer would die a slow, painful death of disease because it was attached to him or her.

As horrific as this sounds, this type of punishment is very similar to how Christians suffer when they struggle with forgiving themselves. Their hearts have been made new through salvation, yet because they carry such deep regret, the dead man of sin is always tied to them.

2 Corinthians 5:17 says, *"Therefore, if anyone is in Christ, he is a new creation; old things have passed away; behold, all things have become new."* When I gave my heart to Jesus, I became new. The word *new* literally means new in kind, describing something which has never existed before. The term "old things" (also referred to as the "old man" or "old self") is a reference to our past life, which is marked by sin and separation from our Heavenly Father.

In God's eyes, when we received Christ as our Savior, the old, guilty man of sin died—hence, the term "passed away." But herein lies the first problem: God never asked us to pick up the dead man.

When I gave my heart to God and became new in Christ, I couldn't seem to forgive the old "me"—much less understand God's forgiveness—so I unknowingly created my own punishment. Like someone found guilty of a crime, I picked up the guilt, the shame, and the unworthiness associated with my old self and carried it around with me everywhere I went.

So although I was born-again, meaning I had given my heart to Jesus and become new on the inside, my mind and emotions constantly suffered a slow, painful demise from the guilt and shame I carried around. And honestly, this self-affliction is a major reason countless people have struggled in their relationship with God.

You may be one of them.

Perhaps, you've confused conviction and condemnation, and therefore don't realize the guilt you are carrying around is not from God and is only weighing you down unnecessarily. The Bible says, *"God has passed over the sins that were previously committed" (Romans 3:25),* meaning when you gave your heart to Jesus, God passed over all the sins of your former life as if they had never occurred. He forgave your sins and according to Hebrews 10:17, which says, *"their sins and lawless deeds, I will remember no more,"* He also forgot them.

Conviction is how God corrects us.

Condemnation is how the devil defeats us.

However, if you don't know, or accept these truths, your life and emotions can look a lot like a gerbil on a wheel, spinning round and round between feelings of guilt and condemnation and attempts to be a better Christian.

Don't Run Around Naked

Ephesians 4:22-24 instructs us to *"...put off, concerning your former conduct, the old man which grows corrupt according to the deceitful lusts, and be renewed in the spirit of your mind, and put on the new man which was created according to God, in true righteousness and holiness."* In this passage, we are told to "put off" our former conduct and "put on" the new nature given to us by Christ. Both require action.

For the most part, we know how to put off the old

behavior. In other words, we have a good idea of what we shouldn't be doing anymore. (Hint: no more lewd talk or inappropriate or immoral behavior, etc.) But because we are daily tempted by our old habits, what we really struggle with is how to put on (and wear) our new identity in Christ.

Before I learned who I was in Christ and how God saw me, my Christian walk revolved around trying *not* to do the things from my past. I had had a horrible potty-mouth! And without meaning to, I would cuss every time I got mad or frustrated. But what was worse was the guilt I felt afterward. I didn't have any idea how to put on and confidently become this "new person" the Bible talked about. I had a desire to leave my former conduct behind me, but I found it difficult. As a result, I constantly felt ashamed and inferior, not realizing that these were tools of the enemy to keep me quiet about my faith in Christ.

So, *spiritually speaking*, between putting off the old man and not yet putting on the new, *I was running around naked!* Now how do naked people act? How would you and I act if we were literally sitting in a room together naked? We would be shifting in our seat attempting to cover ourselves—not unlike how Adam and Eve did when they committed the first sin. The Bible says they hid from God in their shame and nakedness.

The point I am trying to make is that when we only learn how to put off the old man (our old habits and sins), but never learn how to wear the new, we are spiritually naked. And naked people look for covering.

Adam and Eve covered themselves with fig leaves because it was the closest thing they could find. And many times the closest thing a Christian can find when he or she feels naked is their *old* clothes—or we could say, their old behavior.

So the vicious cycle begins.

We have a desire to walk closer with God so we put off the old man. But because we don't know how to put on the new man God created for us in *true righteousness* (versus false or self-righteousness, which we'll explore later), we find ourselves feeling naked, so to speak. We end up retreating to our old behavior because, according to our emotions, that's better than the feeling of being unclothed. But it doesn't take long before we feel guilty for caving in to the old man, so we throw him off again... repeating the cycle over and over.

And eventually, if this process continues long enough, we stop putting off the old nature altogether and just carry it around in the form of masked guilt. And this is exactly what the devil wants you and I to do. Remember, his best-laid plan is for us to defeat ourselves.

However, there is a key to wearing our new identity instead of running around naked or staying stuck in the old. Look at our scripture again: *"...put off, concerning your former conduct, the old man which grows corrupt according to the deceitful lusts, **and be renewed in the spirit of your mind**, and put on the new man which was created according to God, in true righteousness and holiness."*

The key is in renewing our minds.

Consider this: we put on a shirt one step at a time. First one arm... then another arm... and then over the head. In the same way, you can learn to wear your new identity in Christ by renewing your mind one step at a time through *knowledge, confession* and *faith.*

New Clothes

When God put me in front of my mirror, I received knowledge of His love and forgiveness. Then the Holy Spirit prompted me to confess God's Word every time I felt defeated. And finally, I came to a point where I believed God's Word despite how I felt.

Knowledge. Confession. Faith.

These are the keys to renewing our mind and thus, wearing the new clothes God has provided for us. The Bible says, *"I will greatly rejoice in the Lord, my soul shall be joyful in my God; For He has clothed me with the garments of salvation, He has covered me with the robe of righteousness"* (Isaiah 60:10).

First, you have to learn the truths of your righteousness. Then you must build your belief system by agreeing with God's Word (learning to say what God says about you). And lastly, there must be a firmness of belief. These three keys are vital when it comes to growing and maturing as a believer. But in order to break out of the vicious cycle of guilt, shame, and inferiority, you need to make a decision right now if you are going to believe God's Word—not just part of it, but all of it.

Hard-To-Grasp Truth

For example, you need to know God's Word regarding your right-standing in Christ because condemnation is a mean trick of the devil. He knows God is full of grace and mercy and will forgive your sins, so he lies to you and plants suggestive thoughts in your mind that are contrary to God's Word. These thoughts build up walls that keep the life God intended for you locked on the outside—out of your reach.

The mortar of these walls can be a combination of many things: such as insecurities, failures, disappointments, and fears, all of which stem from your own inability to love, forgive and accept yourself as God does. And even though you and I can read about—or hear great sermons about—God's awesome forgiveness, *each time you look in the mirror your reflection will speak differently.*

When I finally forgave myself, all 100-something pounds of guilt and condemnation (the equivalent of the "old" me) dropped to the ground. I had become so accustomed to carrying guilt and shame around that I didn't realize the heaviness of it. Paul said, *"Our old man was crucified with Him, that the body of sin might be done away with, that we should no longer be slaves of sin" (Romans 6:6).* In other words, we don't have to be a slave to who we *once* were.

The hard-to-grasp truth for any of us is that our sins were crucified with Jesus. This means we don't have to be a slave to them anymore. But just like the convicted murderer in days of old, as long as you and I continue to hold on to the dead junk of our past, it will hinder where we go, what we do, and how we feel about ourselves.

Mulan asked a very good question indeed, "When will my reflection show who I am *inside*?" I believe the answer is first found in understanding and accepting God's truth.

Chapter Four

Cricket Mentalities

I don't think of all the misery but of all the beauty that still remains.
-Anne Frank

Here's a statement that might make you think:

How we view ourselves will always have a greater impact on us than how we view God.

Think about it... How do you view God?

Now, in comparison, how do you view yourself?

More than likely, how you view yourself is how you live your life. In other words, no matter what you've heard or read, or even positively believed about God, when you stand in front of your mirror, what you think about yourself has a greater impact on your life.

Children of God (or Grasshoppers?)

In the Book of Numbers, Chapter 13, we find a good

illustration of this tendency. God said to Moses, *"Send men to spy out the land of Canaan, which I am giving to the children of Israel" (verse 2).* His directive was clear. God wanted tried-and-true leaders to spy out the land He would give them as an inheritance. He didn't ask Moses or the people to *judge* the land to see if they could or could not take it. His request for them to scout out the land was simply so they could see it for themselves.

Yet when the twelve spies returned from their mission, only two believed God's original word. The others all said, *"There we saw the giants (the descendants of Anak...); and we were like grasshoppers in our own sight and so we were in their sight" (verse 33).*

Notice it was how they viewed themselves that overrode what God had said and promised to them.

The same is still true today. In fact, I dare say this story gives us a good percentage of the typical number of people who wrestle with self-worth: ten out of twelve. If true, more than 80% of the common population struggle with insecurities, self-doubt, and inferiority issues. Now, how many of those are Christians —children of God?

The Bible contains numerous descriptions of God's love for us, and how He sees us. I once heard someone say, "God's greatest joy is to be believed. His greatest pain is to be doubted." God desires for us to understand and accept His promises for ourselves, but in a similar manner to how God's children judged the land, many people judge their mirror based on how *they* feel and what *they* think, instead of what God has said.

Instead of believing God's Word, they have determined they are "like grasshoppers" in their own sight, and thus, must be in God's sight.

Kenneth E. Hagin once made this statement: "You see, a lot of times, our thinking is wrong. It's not in line with the Bible. And if our thinking is wrong, then our believing is going to be wrong. And if our believing is wrong, then our talking is going to be wrong. You've got to get all three of them—your thinking, your believing, and your speaking—synchronized with the Word of God."

This is so true of a large majority of the Body of Christ. We don't realize our thinking isn't in line with God's

Word. But Jesus said it's not hard to locate what we believe: *"For out of the abundance of the heart the mouth speaks" (Matthew 12:34).* All we have to do is listen to what we say and we'll know what we believe. The spies revealed their belief system when they said, *"We [are] like grasshoppers."*

Wrong thinking leads to a wrong belief system; a wrong belief system leads to wrong speaking, and this is where we get in a mess. Jesus said if a man *"...believes that those things (he says) will be done, he will have whatever he says" (Mark 11:23b).* We prefer to look at this scripture in the positive, but it doesn't read "You'll have only the *right and good* things you believe and say."

Unfortunately, it works in the negative as well. Every word we speak strengthens and empowers our belief system—right or wrong.

Sealed Fate

I once heard a story about a young boy who had caught a handful of crickets and put them in a wide-mouth jar. Inside the jar he placed your typical supplies, such as grass, flies, and berries. Then he put a lid on the jar with several holes punched in the top for air. Immediately, the crickets began jumping hysterically trying to get out of the jar only to hit the lid and bounce back down. This behavior went on for a couple of days and then suddenly stopped.

Contrary to their previous behavior, the crickets became content within their jar, moving about inside it, eating and adapting to their new surroundings.

When the boy removed the lid, the crickets didn't notice. Curious to see what would happen, he left the lid off the jar but the crickets never tried to escape. Before, they had tried to get out only to be beaten down. Now that they could leave, they contently stayed. Why? Because in the process of time, they had programmed themselves to believe their fate was sealed.

Many of us are like these crickets.

Proverbs 4:23 says, *"Keep your heart with all diligence, for out of it spring the issues of life."* In other words, be careful what you believe. If you believe you are a failure, an outcast, or unworthy, you will believe your "jar" is your fate, when in reality it is nothing but a barrier to the truth.

"Keep (or guard) your heart with all diligence, for OUT OF IT spring the issues of life." Whatever belief system you put in your heart is what will come out. And whatever comes out of your heart is the picture you'll believe. For example, when the crickets no longer believed there was an escape, they stopped trying to find one.

In the same way, others can tell you the truth and even point to freedom, but if you don't believe it, you will never attempt it—no matter how good it sounds. I'll remind you again: *"For as a man thinks in his heart, so is he"* (Proverbs 23:7a).

The Hebrew word for issues in Proverbs 4:23 is literally translated as boundaries or controlling factors. So the Psalmist is saying, *"Keep (or guard) your heart with all diligence, for out it spring the [boundaries or controlling factors] of life."* When someone beats us down with their words or treats us with contempt or prejudice, we tend to fight back at first.

> *It is what a man thinks of himself that really determines his fate.*
> -Henry David Thoreau

But over time, the fight can get tiresome, and little by little, we begin to adjust our life to fit within the lie. Therefore, (often unknowingly) the words and actions of others, and then our own words and actions build an invisible prison.

Miserable and Lost

I have a friend who heads up a large ministry for people who struggle with sexual issues.[1] He is able to help these individuals because he himself came out of a homosexual lifestyle. When he was younger, some older boys in his neighborhood called him "fag" and other horrible names because he wasn't athletic or noticeably strong. Then, in a separate incident, he was molested by a boy in a pretend game of "doctor." As the years passed, he wondered to himself if maybe he was gay. He didn't feel he was, but the words and actions of others had planted seeds in his heart.

When he entered college, he met some openly gay people and gravitated toward them, still wondering if this was his identity also. Several years later, miserable and lost, he found his way to the ministry he now leads.

The words and actions of others, and then his own words and actions, built an invisible prison that not only confined him, but also *defined* him. After learning the truth and reversing what he believed about himself, my friend is now happily married and helping others find the truth of who they are in Christ according to God's Word.

But there are countless men and women today living in invisible prisons similar to my friend's or even my own "glass box." Many were raised in Christian homes where they attended church regularly at an early age. Others, like myself, did not begin having a relationship with God until they were adults. Yet in either case, both can have feelings programmed to believe God is unreachable and their sins are too great. The problem lies within. Their mindset is contrary to God's thoughts and they simply lack knowledge of their identity in Christ.

And if asked to give a reason for their feelings, most of these strugglers would likely say, "I don't know why," while some might say, "Well, I've made a lot of mistakes..." Both statements contain an element of truth and give an explanation for their struggle.

For example, when someone says they don't know why they feel the way they do, they are simply admitting they don't have the answer. They really don't know. Now consider this: God said in Hosea 4:6, *"My people are destroyed for a lack of knowledge."* In other words, having a lack of knowledge is the same as not having the answer, and the result is destruction.

Similarly, when someone feels distant from God and believes their mistakes are the reason why, the same is true: *they are being destroyed by a lack of knowledge.* They have allowed their understanding of sin to outweigh their understanding of God's love and forgiveness.

The biggest danger with either of these mindsets is that it is a playground for the enemy. In Second Corinthians 2:11, the Bible says, *"Lest Satan take advantage of us, we are not ignorant of his devices."* Ignorance is not stupidity. The definition of ignorance is a lack of knowledge. This explains a lot.

God's people are destroyed because of ignorance; and in that condition, Satan takes advantage of us.

We've all made mistakes. But it's the memory of them that often hinders us. God said, *"Their sins and their lawless deeds I will remember no more" (Hebrews 10:17).* Yet we remember them—and our enemy, the devil, wants to make sure we remember them. So, because our past failures and disappointments linger on the forefront of our mind, they then compound with every small or large mistake in our present life, making us feel continually unworthy of God's love and forgiveness. Then based on the lies fueled by our own ignorance, we become programmed to a failure mentality.

The Scale is Tipped

In my ignorance and inferiority, I constantly asked God to forgive me of the same sins over and over. I was guilty of meditating on my past and the things I had done before salvation—never realizing I was only adding to the mortar of my invisible prison. My early years of Christianity consisted of a vicious cycle of wrong meditation and pitiful prayer.

But in an effort to be freed from my jar of condemnation, I kept this up—continually asking God to forgive me of my previous sins, forgetting, not believing, or simply not fully realizing, He had already forgiven me when I received Jesus as my Lord. Then, because I thought Christians had to be perfect, my feelings of unworthiness were multiplied by my day-to-day failures. I was like an unbalanced scale.

Have you ever seen a two-sided scale? They are rare today, but a long time ago they were frequently used in commerce and trade. For example, a gold miner would lay his treasure on one side of the scale while the banker laid the weights on the other side to determine the value of his gold. The banker would put an *equal* amount of weight opposite the gold until the scale was balanced.

I compare my early self to an unbalanced scale because one side was filled with a *limited* knowledge of my identity in Christ. The other side of the scale tipped way over with my *full* knowledge of sin. This lopsided understanding was the reason for the deception in my life and resulted in compounded guilt and condemnation, and a belief that I would never be able to fully earn God's love.

So instead of feeling closer to God when I asked for His forgiveness for my sins and failures, I always felt more distanced (and out of balance). But the Bible says, *"The Lord is gracious and full of compassion..." (Psalm 145:8)*. His desire is for every person to be saved and come to the knowledge of truth (1 Timothy 2:4).

God doesn't just want us to be saved; He wants us to *walk*, *live*, and *flourish* in His love.

Chapter Five

The Truth About God

You can bend it and twist it... You can misuse and abuse it... But even God cannot change the Truth.
-Michael Levy

In the famous children's novel, <u>*Alice in Wonderland*</u>,[1] the Queen of Hearts is an interesting character. Overseeing the kingdom with the King of Hearts, she changes from pleasant to enraged every other minute. At the slightest offense, she shouts, "Off with their heads!" It seems ordering executions is one of her hobbies. However, as the story goes, very few were actually beheaded. The kind King of Hearts quietly pardoned many of his subjects while his foul-tempered wife wasn't looking.

King of Hearts

This story makes me wonder about how people see God. Do they view Him as a quick-to-judge King who enjoys shelling out punishment like the Queen of Hearts? Or do they see Him as the kind King of Hearts pardoning the offenses of His subjects?

The Apostle Paul asked, *"Don't you see how wonderfully kind, tolerant, and patient God is with you? Does this mean nothing to you? Can't you see that His kindness is intended to turn you from your sin" (Romans 2:4)?* [2] It's hard to determine exactly how people form their opinion of God—maybe they had a hard father or a moody mother. In those cases, I could almost understand a misguided view of God since our earthly parents are sometimes the only example we have—*right or wrong.*

When I was growing up, I had a friend who was raised in a very strict Christian home. She often wanted to spend the night at my house because our rules were quite different and she could do what she wanted without consequence. Years later, when we were in college and I had become a Christian, we bumped into each other and I was very excited to share my new-found faith with her. But to my surprise, she had abandoned her beliefs.

She explained that if God was as hard as her parents made Him out to be, she'd rather spend her life enjoying herself. I didn't know the harsh "God" she spoke of, so I left our conversation very sad.

The God I met and fell in love with was a King of Hearts. Despite all my failures and extreme sins, He pardoned me. And the more realization I've had of how much He actually pardoned, the more I love Him and want to serve Him. The Bible says, *"[When] we were foolish and disobedient, we were misled and became slaves to many lusts and pleasures. Our lives were full of evil and envy, and we hated each other. But when God our Savior revealed His kindness and love, He saved us, not because of the righteous things we had done, but because of His mercy" (Titus 3:3-5).*

If I were to compare someone to the Queen of Hearts, it sure wouldn't be God. **Despite all my mistakes, I've yet to hear Him say, "Off with her head!"** Instead, His kindness has been generous and His love unfailing. This is why the Bible says, *"God demonstrated His own love toward us, in that while we were still sinners, Christ died for us" (Romans 5:8).*

He is the King of Hearts and *"...with undeserved kindness, He declares that we [who put our trust in Him now] to be righteous. And He did this through Christ Jesus when He freed us from the penalty of our sins"* (Romans 3:24).

We need to fully understand: **There was a penalty.** *But there was also a payment.* When the order should have been, "Off with their heads!"—a new and superior order was made: *"Restore them to Me!"* The King spoke it, and His Word was fulfilled. Not based on anything we have or haven't done, His grace covers a multitude of sin. *"For if we are saved by God's kindness, then it is not by our good works. For in that case, God's wonderful kindness would not be what it really is—free and undeserved"* (Romans 11:6). [3]

The truth is, He is the King of kindness and for that reason He has become the King of my heart. 1 John 4:8 says, *"...God is love."* In fact, not only did He demonstrate His love by sending His Son to rescue us, but the Bible says He did it *"...while we were of no use whatsoever to him."* [4]

God is Love

In other words, when we were offensive, repulsive and full of error, God still demonstrated His Love. *"For God so loved the world that He gave His only begotten Son... (John 3:16)."*

I want you to think about that. Really consider it. God demonstrated His

> *Whenever you have truth it must be given with love, or the message and the messenger will be rejected.*
>
> -Mahatma Gandhi

Love [Himself] for us by sending Jesus to die while we were up to our necks in sin. So why do some people (maybe even you) believe He is out to get us now? If God wanted to reject us, He could've done it before sending Jesus to die for our sins. But He didn't *because He loves us.*

So if God is LOVE, what does He look like? One way to see God's true character is to substitute the word *love* with the word *God* in scripture. For example, the passages in First Corinthians 13:4-7, often known as the "Love Chapter," would read this way:

> *[God] is patient and kind. [God] is not jealous or boastful or proud or rude. [God] does not demand [His] own way. [God] is not irritable, and keeps no record of being wronged. [God] does not rejoice about*

injustice but rejoices whenever the truth wins out.

[God] never gives up, never loses faith, is always

hopeful, and endures through every circumstance. [5]

These are the marks and attributes of our God. This is how He was toward us when we got saved and it is how He still is toward us now!

He is patient and kind. He is not impatient or cruel when we mess up. *He is not jealous or boastful or proud or rude,* meaning He is not jealous of "other gods" in our life (such as television, sports, or even our family). But He does love us with a jealous love because He wants to be number one in our lives. And we can count on Him to be trusting, modest, humble and polite.

God doesn't demand His own way. He simply requests and then waits to see what we choose. *He is also not irritable, and He keeps no record of being wronged.* Instead, He is tolerant and He forgives and forgets.

The devil wants us to believe He is hard and demanding and apt to strike us with lightening if (and when) we make a mistake. But that's not the truth. Psalms 146:8 says, *"The Lord opens the eyes of the blind; The Lord raises those who are bowed down; The Lord loves the righteous."* To be bowed down describes a person who is crouched in spirit—broken and hurting. The righteous is the term He uses for His children. What kind of Father would He be if He responded negatively to His children who are broken and hurting?

Yet people everywhere have believed He despises them because of their sin. It is true that God hates wickedness, but He doesn't hate us. Even when we were trespassers before salvation, full of wickedness because our lives had not yet been redeemed, He demonstrated His love for us.

This is why *God never gives up, never loses faith, and is always hopeful...* In other words, He sees our potential. He saw it before salvation and He still sees it now.

He's a Good Father

Because of His Love, God is called our Father. You may not have had an earthly father who demonstrated this kind of love, but don't let that be a reflection of your Heavenly Father. The devil is the one trying to keep you from drawing close to Him by comparing the two. No matter how good your earthly father was or is, there's still no comparison!

"See what [an incredible] quality of love the Father has given (shown, bestowed on) us, that we should [be permitted to] be named and called and counted as the children of God! And so we are" (1 John 3:1).[6] Jesus called God His Father because He was His Son. But Jesus also called Him "Father" because of His Love. After His resurrection, Jesus told Mary Magdalene to tell everyone, *"I am ascending to* **My** *Father and* **your** *Father, and to* **My** *God and* **your** *God" (John 20:17).*

Jesus wanted to make sure we knew we were included. We could've been left as orphans, but instead we were adopted and brought into the family of God. And this is why John said, *"We love Him, because He first loved us" (1 John 4:19).*

He's a Good Shepherd

One day I was meditating on several passages of scripture that speak of God being like a shepherd. As I did, the Holy Spirit gave me this short story:

When the little lamb was born, it looked to its mother for nourishment and safety. The mother taught the little lamb how to graze and find food and water. As the lamb grew, it became more and more independent from its mother. Most of his days were spent with its head down grazing and rarely did the little lamb look up. His mother had warned him of dangers that loomed near the thicket, but the little lamb had never been face-to-face with real danger so his mother's warnings seemed insignificant. *Until one day...*

The wolf eyed the little lamb from the edge of the thicket. He noticed how independent he had become, and therefore vulnerable. As the lamb slowly moved closer and closer to the edge of the thicket with his head down grazing on the lush grass, the wolf planned its attack.

Suddenly, the lamb was scooped up and hoisted into the air! Within seconds, the little lamb was in the embrace of the Shepherd and saved from ultimate destruction.

This is a beautiful comparison to my life, and probably yours. I was ignorant and unaware, but God was watching over me nonetheless. *"For you were like sheep going astray, but have now returned to the Shepherd and Overseer of your souls" (1 Peter 2:25).* For the most part, our parents, or earthly caregivers, did their best to nurture and keep us safe for a season—even warning us of looming danger—but in our ignorance, we kept our head down focused on our immediate needs and wants, oblivious of the wolf *or the Shepherd.*

When my brother became a Christian, he excitedly tried to tell me about salvation but I thought it was silliness. I was too consumed with my so-called life. But now I'm glad God was patient and merciful. In fact, I am in awe that He still stood by ready and willing to rescue me even after I had rejected Him.

Ignorance can be a killer. Some people are ignorant of God's love. Others are ignorant of His mercy. While others, are just plain ignorant of His salvation period.

Thankfully, the *"Shepherd and Overseer of our souls"* isn't offended easily. He is rejected everyday, yet that doesn't stop Him from loving us. In fact, when God saw our condition—because He's a good Father and full of love and mercy—He made a plan of rescue. *"This is what the Almighty Lord says: I will search for my sheep myself, and I will look after them. As a shepherd looks after his flock when he is with his scattered sheep, so I will look after my sheep. I will rescue them on a cloudy and gloomy day from every place where they have been scattered"* (Ezekiel 34:11-12).

One component of mercy is a desire to make things right. When our heads were down, *God had mercy.* When danger loomed nearby, *God had mercy.* When we should have been destroyed, *God had mercy.*

"Like a shepherd He takes care of his flock. He gathers the lambs in his arms. He carries them in his arms. He gently helps the sheep and their lambs" (Isaiah 40:11).

Sometimes children, who are naturally ignorant of the dangers of this world, lose their innocence at a young age simply because they weren't protected by their caregivers. In fact, sometimes it is the caregiver themselves who inflict the pain on their young through direct contact; or second-handedly because they are so consumed with their own pain that the young are left neglected, confused, and exposed to outside influences. And this unfortunate cycle can continue for many generations.

But the Bible says God delivers us in His righteousness and causes us to escape (Psalm 71:2). I realize now God didn't just deliver and rescue me on the day I was saved. He also delivered me in front of my mirror; He rescued me as He opened up my understanding of His Word and as He revealed Himself in tangible ways.

But the truth is, if I believed He was hard and judgmental, I know I'd still be in bondage today—*perfect prey for the wolf.*

So whatever you have believed up until this point about God, I sincerely hope you are beginning to recognize how much He truly loves you. Your thinking may be small, but your God is big.

Chapter Six

A Permanent Solution

*The supreme happiness of life is the conviction
that we are loved.*
-Victor Hugo

In 1864, Abraham Lincoln wrote a letter to the widow Lydia Bixby in condolence for the loss of her five sons in battle.[1] Although the letter is now debated as a piece of literature, there is no argument as *to whom*, and *for what reason*, the letter was written.

In Peter's second letter to Christians everywhere, he addressed it in this manner: *"To those who have obtained like precious faith with us by the righteousness of our God and Savior Jesus Christ" (2 Peter 1:1).* Although read by many today, Peter was writing to a specific group, for a specific reason.

It seems he assumed Christians reading his letter understood (and had faith in) God's gift of righteousness to all believers. Yet, interestingly, many people today—

to whom this timeless letter is still written—do not have faith in, much less understanding of, the righteousness he is referring to.

Yet the Bible says, *"For He made Him who knew no sin to be sin for us, that we might become the righteousness of God in Him" (2 Corinthians 5:21).* In other words, God made Jesus (who had never sinned) to become the carrier of sin for us (who were burdened with sin) so that we might become (upon accepting Him as our Savior) the righteousness of God in Him.

This one scripture describes the great exchange Jesus did on our behalf—it means we literally traded places. For this reason, all references to who we are *in Christ* are directly related to who God has made us to be through the death and resurrection of His Son. So from this passage alone, we learn we are *"the righteousness of God in Him."* In other words, Jesus became sin... we became righteous.

And our righteousness is both a position and a corresponding action.

But before we get into all that, let's back up and look at

how righteousness got its start. It will make more sense if we take a closer look at God's original plan for man.

Everything Began with Relationship

You know the story: Genesis explains how God created man for fellowship. Adam and Eve walked daily in the garden with God. They talked to Him, listened to Him, and simply spent time in His presence. They were close to God. In other words, they could reach Him. And the Bible says God was very pleased with His creation of mankind.

The serpent however, who was Satan himself, didn't like this relationship between man and God so he plotted to deceive Adam and Eve into disobeying God by eating of the tree of knowledge of good and evil of which God had commanded them not to eat.[2] When they did, sin (defined as disobedience to God's commands) entered the world for the very first time and suddenly, the utopia of the Garden of Eden was lost.

"And [when] they heard the sound of the Lord God walking in the garden in the cool of the day, Adam and his wife hid themselves from the presence of the Lord God among the

trees of the garden. Then the Lord God called to Adam and said to him, 'Where are you?' So he said, 'I heard Your voice in the garden, and I was afraid because I was naked; and I hid myself'" (Genesis 3:8-10).

Adam and Eve were hiding in shame because that's what sin does —it causes us to withdraw from God. From that point on, because of sin and its consequences, mankind was separated from their Creator. And without a plan to cover sin, man would never be able to reach God again.

Adam and Eve were very grieved by their sin. And I dare say you can relate because most likely you've been grieved at one point or another by your mistakes.

But Adam and Eve weren't the only ones heartbroken. God was also very saddened by this turn of events. But in His mercy the Lord designed a plan to cleanse humans from their sins through the use of their most precious commodity: *blood.* Without it, none of us can live.

But God made it more precious than just a substance that circulates in the human body in order to live. Hebrews 9:22 says, *"According to the law of Moses, nearly everything was purified with blood. For without the shedding of blood, there is no forgiveness."* [3] And Leviticus explains: *"For the life of the body is in its blood. And I [the Lord] have given you the blood on the altar to purify you, making you right with the Lord. It is the blood, given in exchange for a life, that makes purification possible."* [4]

After the fall of Adam and Eve, God required the blood of bulls and goats to be offered to Him in order for sins to be washed from His sight. But there was still a problem.

This didn't completely remedy the broken relationship between God and man —*"for it's not possible that the blood of bulls and goats could take away sins" (Hebrews 10:4).* Much like placing a rug over your stained carpet, the blood offering merely *covered* the sins. It temporarily hid them but was never a permanent solution.

But God had another plan at work. Back on that fateful day in the Garden of Eden, God said something interesting to Satan: *"From now on, you and the woman will be enemies, as will your offspring and hers. You will strike his heel, but He will crush your head" (Genesis 3:15).*

This one statement gave a hint as to what to expect next. God had designed a temporary solution through the blood of bulls and goats, but His real (and permanent) plan of rescue would be through another means.

Fractured

When I was in the 2nd Grade, I stepped out into the street without looking and was hit by a car. Besides the sheer trauma of the event and some broken teeth, I also fractured my right ankle at the growth plate. A fracture is simply a break, or something left in a state of being broken. The doctors had to place a cast on my leg from my toes to my hip to make sure nothing moved while the bone healed. This was a long process that required me to be wheelchair-bound for almost a year, but thankfully today, both my legs are the same length and I am strong—all because of the cast that was placed on my leg.

In a similar picture, when sin entered the world, we were separated from God causing our relationship to be fractured. Yet the Bible speaks of how God reconciled the world to Himself. *"For it pleased the Father that in Him all the fullness should dwell, and by Him to* **reconcile** *all things to Himself, by Him, whether things on earth or things in Heaven, having made peace through the Blood of His Cross"* (Colossians 1:19-20).

The word "reconcile" simply means to re-establish a fractured relationship. God's plan of reconciliation was for Jesus to be the cast, in order to heal what had been fractured. *"But now in Christ Jesus you who once were far off* (fractured) *have been brought near* (reconciled) *by the Blood of Christ"* (Ephesians 2:13, emphasis added). The Blood of Jesus became the permanent solution to man's separation problem, whereas the blood of bulls and goats had only been a band-aid.

I like the way the New Living Translation explains the reconciliation Jesus made for us: *"So Christ has now become the High Priest over all the good things that have come. He has entered that greater, more perfect Tabernacle in Heaven, which was not made by human hands and is not part of this created world. With His own blood—not the blood of goats and calves—He entered the Most Holy Place once for all time and secured our redemption forever. Under the old system, the blood of*

goats and bulls and the ashes of a young cow could
cleanse people's bodies from ceremonial impurity. Just
think how much more the Blood of Christ will purify our
consciences from sinful deeds so that we can worship the
living God. For by the power of the eternal Spirit, Christ
offered Himself to God as a perfect sacrifice for our sins.
That is why He is the one who mediates the new covenant
between God and people, so that all who are called can
receive the eternal inheritance God has promised them.
For Christ died to set them free from the penalty of the sins
they had committed under that first covenant" (Hebrews
9:11-15).[5]

What a plan! God is now able to receive us and forgive
our sins because of the sacrifice made by Jesus.
Therefore, He no longer sees us as sinners, beggars, or
outcasts. When we accept Jesus as our Savior, God sees
us through His blood. And this is key because the Bible
says God was pleased to offer forgiveness by the blood of
Christ, *"...to demonstrate His righteousness" (Romans*
3:25).

And that's not all. Have you ever been in a playful
wrestling match where you, or your opponent, yelled

"Uncle!" in order to be released? This might be another good picture of how God reconciled us. We were held tight in the grip of sin as a pawn of Satan, but Jesus reconciled us back to God (by making the devil yell "Uncle!"). Satan had no intention of letting us go, but Jesus overpowered him. And He did this by making peace through the blood of His cross. And peace is actually a synonym for the word reconciliation. In other words, Jesus made peace (meaning He reconciled God and man) through His blood sacrifice.

Be Aware of Satan's Devices

But be warned: Satan is still up to his old tricks. He will use anything he can to deceive us,

> *No man was ever so deceived by another as by himself.*
> -Author Unknown

including insecurities, feelings of low self-worth, fears, failures, regrets and disappointments. His goal is to separate us from walking in the fullness of God's plan. Remember, *"Lest Satan should take advantage of us; ...we [should not be] ignorant of his devices"* (2 Corinthians 2:11).

Satan knows how we see ourselves is a key element to

our relationship with God. His goal is to get us to re-think if we are truly worthy to walk closely with the God of the universe. Our struggles always boil down to how we view ourselves—which always has a greater impact on our lives than how we view God.

His Righteousness

So what is this righteousness God has supposedly established us in? In Chapter Three, we looked at Ephesians 4:24, where the Apostle Paul explained how the new man in Christ was *"...created according to God, in **true** righteousness and holiness..."* I love this because it first indicates this was God's idea.

Therefore, righteousness (our right-standing with God) was never a plan devised by man. It was the forethought of our Heavenly Father. In fact, Psalm 11:7 says, *"For the Lord is righteous, He loves righteousness; His countenance beholds the upright."* In another place, the Bible says, *"He shall judge the world in righteousness, and He shall administer judgment for the peoples in uprightness"* (Psalm 9:8). No wonder King David prayed, *"Lead me, O Lord, in Your righteousness..." (Psalm 5:8).*

It seems that just as 2+2 = 4, righteousness is the sum of God's desire and God's direction for our lives.

If we will allow it to lead and direct us, then we can rest assure we are in the center of God's will. And I believe this is what you, and every other Christian, desires. God never intended for any of us to live on a roller-coaster of doubt and insecurity.

Isaiah prophesied regarding: *"The voice of one crying in the wilderness: [saying] 'Prepare the way of the Lord; make straight in the desert a highway for our God. Every valley shall be exalted and every mountain and hill brought low; the crooked places shall be made straight and the rough places smooth "* (Isaiah 40:3-4). Sounds like *non*-roller-coaster living to me!

Of course, we now understand Isaiah was speaking of John the Baptist who became the voice crying out to prepare the way for Jesus. But what path was he speaking of? What task was laid out before Jesus? The Bible says Jesus would *"...become sin that we might become the righteousness of God in Him"* (2 Corinthians

5:21), therefore, John the Baptist was essentially declaring, "Prepare the way for righteousness!"

And the result? *"Every valley shall be exalted and every mountain and hill brought low; the crooked places shall be made straight and the rough places smooth."*

Watch Your Step

So the righteousness God created and prepared for mankind was made through Jesus. In fact, the Psalmist said, *"Righteousness will go before Him, and shall make His footsteps our pathway" (Psalm 85:13).* This is why Jesus declared, *"I am the Way..."* [6]

We could liken this picture to a minefield. If it were necessary for us to cross a certain plot of land to reach our destination, yet we knew the land was covered in fatal mines, it would be wise for us to follow the footsteps of those who had safely crossed to the other side. **Righteousness has made His footsteps our pathway.** The world can be a dangerous place, but we can safely maneuver through it by walking in the path of righteousness.

Purely by definition, righteousness is right-standing with God, including the ability to stand before Him without guilt or inferiority as if you had never sinned. It was given to us at the new birth (when we were born-again) and it continues with us as we continue with God. This is why the scripture says, *"If you confess your sins, He is faithful and just to forgive you and cleanse you of all unrighteousness" (1 John 1:9).* God didn't provide righteousness for us just to watch us lose it the first time we fall into sin. But He also didn't provide it as an excuse and cover-up for our sin either.

Righteousness is the system of forgiveness and cleansing of our sin in order to bring us into the presence and fellowship of God Himself. This was His plan and it is still His desire.

But we must be careful. When reading the Book of Job, we find that he became a little confused on this subject and his misunderstandings are written in God's Word as a warning and help to us. In fact, after listening for some time to Job's rantings, his friend Elihu asked him, *"Do you think this is right? Do you say 'my righteousness' is more than God's" (Job 35:2)?* More than likely, Job didn't intentionally set out to be high-minded. He probably just slipped over there because of deception (and ignorance). But if he misunderstood God's righteousness, so can we.

The point is, if we'll follow the footsteps of Jesus, learning to stand in the presence of God without guilt and inferiority over our past, or prideful and high-minded because of our good works, our lives will be more than we ever imagined. The bottom line is: *righteousness only changes us… not God* –just like our sins only affect us, not Him. God remains the same and His provision for us remains unchanged as well.

Ultimately, Job's friend summed up his faith this way: *"I will fetch my knowledge from afar; I will ascribe righteousness to my Maker" (Job 36:3).* The word "ascribe" simply means to give credit to something or someone. Elihu understood righteousness is a concept far beyond our natural understanding, yet without hesitation we should attribute it to God, its originator, and receive it gratefully. It's an indescribable gift, with amazing benefits.

Chapter Seven

The Free Gift

God's gifts put man's best dreams to shame.
-Elizabeth Barret

Have you ever received a gift that was hard to accept? One that was really over-the-top, something which you felt very undeserving of? *I have*—on many occasions actually. It's a two-fold issue for me. One, I have a strong work ethic so I often feel I can only receive things I have worked hard for. But secondly, I struggle with not feeling worthy of such generosity.

One time in particular, I remember receiving a gift from a friend of mine who was always quite generous. She often bought me things as random acts of kindness. I was a young mom and money was very tight in our home. She was single and a career woman with extra to spend. I didn't realize how much I struggled with receiving until one day she said to me, "Don't rob me of a blessing!"

Her words have stuck with me to this day—especially

now that I'm able to be the giver. There is such joy in being able to bless others, for no particular reason, other than just because you can and it was on your heart to do so.

God feels the same way.

We know God is a giver. *"For God so loved the world that He **gave** His only begotten Son so that whoever believes on Him shall not perish but have everlasting life" (John 3:16).* First and foremost, He gave His Son. He gave His very best. Yet people everywhere struggle with receiving this gift of life. Yet, because we are in desperate need of a Savior, many of us accept salvation, but only on conditions we can come to terms with. For example, we'll receive the promise of eternal life (a home in heaven), and to a point, we'll receive forgiveness of sins—just enough to get us saved. But we often wrestle with accepting anything more than that because we feel undeserving.

Learning to Accept His Gift

This was exactly my problem. I had come to a point where I knew I couldn't continue in this life on my own. I believed and was convinced I needed Jesus as my Savior, so if receiving forgiveness of sins is what it took for me to receive eternal life, then I accepted it—*to a point.*

My strong work ethic quickly kicked in causing me to feel I must *earn* my salvation. This soon became a stumbling block in my life. And in addition, the more I learned about God's love and acceptance, the more I struggled with feeling unworthy of His generosity.

In many ways, I could relate more to Adam than to Jesus. The Bible says, *"Therefore, as sin came into the world through one man [Adam], and death as a result of sin, so death spread to all men, [no one being able to stop it or to escape its power] because all men sinned" (Romans 5:12).*[1] One things was for sure, I didn't need to be convinced I was a sinner. This I knew all too well. I was always aware of my sin. *"For I acknowledge my transgressions, and my sin is always before me" (Psalm 51:3).*

Yet after being born-again with the promise of eternal life, I still struggled because I identified more with Adam's sin than with the righteousness Christ exchanged for me. What I didn't understand is that God had given me a *gift*. And not unlike any of the other gifts I had received in my life, I was rejecting it, not feeling worthy or deserving of it.

The sin, which spread from Adam to mankind, was anything but a gift! It was an inherent nature, meaning we were born with it. It isn't a matter of receiving it or not, it is just something every person has from the moment of conception. But what Jesus offers to those who believe is a *true gift*, meaning we are given a choice whether or not to receive it. And His gift is righteousness.

*"For if by the one man's offense death reigned through the one, much more those who receive abundance of grace and of **the gift of righteousness** will reign in life through the One, Jesus Christ" (Romans 5:17).* One translation says, *"...for all who receive [this gift] will live in triumph over sin and death..."* [2] In other words, Jesus wasn't just giving us forgiveness of sins and an identity in Him, He also gave us the ability to triumph over our circumstances through His authority. This is what it means to reign in life!

So this gift of righteousness truly encompasses

everything the believer needs!

Abounded to Many

But surprisingly, the gift of righteousness (given through Jesus) and the offense of sin (given through Adam) have an important similarity. The Bible says they both *"abounded to many."*

We know sin abounded to everyone –from Adam's first child to now. But once Jesus reconciled Himself to the world through the blood of His cross and His resurrection from the dead, righteousness also abounded! And that's where the commonality stops.

*"**The free gift is not like the offense.** For if by the one man's offense many died, much more the grace of God and the gift of grace of the one Man, Jesus Christ, abounded to many. And the gift is not like that which came through the one who sinned. For the judgment which came from one offense resulted in condemnation, but the free gift which came from many offenses resulted in justification"* (Romans 5:15-16).

Did you catch that? One resulted in *condemnation*

(judgment, disapproval, criticism, dishonor, disgrace, and contempt). The other resulted in *justification* (approval, blessing, esteem, acceptance, regard, and respect). No wonder we have struggled with receiving this magnificent gift! The first set of words are easy to identify with; the second set are words we would use to describe our admiration *for Him*—not ourselves.

But another important word derived from the righteousness we've received is *favor*.

Interestingly, this word is often used to describe a token (or gift), given to attendees at a party. The guests aren't the ones being celebrated, yet they receive a "party favor" nonetheless. Or maybe I should say they are "offered" a party favor.

As Christians, we understand Jesus is the One whom we love and celebrate. Yet, He offers all who come to Him something extraordinary—His favor (His gift of righteousness).

Righteous Favor

In the scriptures, we find God showing special favor to

many individuals. One in particular is the special woman chosen to bring Jesus into this world. It seems the only time we speak of the Virgin Mary or gravitate toward her story is during the Christmas holidays, but I have found great revelation through her account regardless of the time of year.

We would all agree she is definitely one who found favor with God. In fact, the angel Gabriel said to her, *"Rejoice, highly favored one, the Lord is with you; blessed are you among women!" (Luke 1:28).*

I'm sure Mary was quite taken aback that an angel was in her room, much less talking to her. But the scriptures say it was "his words" which troubled her the most. *"When she saw him, she was troubled **at his saying**, and considered what manner of greeting this was. Then the angel said to her, 'Do not be afraid, Mary, for you have found favor with God'" (Luke 1:29-30).*

The word *favor* is translated in other places in scripture as acceptance, kindness, great respect, to be loved by another, or to be pleased with. We see the same spoken over Daniel, Jesus, Esther, Ruth, David and many others—and rightly so. From our perspective and vantage point, they all did great things for God and therefore were *deserving* of His favor.

In the dictionary, you will find that favor also means:

1. Something done or granted out of goodwill, rather than from justice; a kindly act.
2. The state of being approved or held in regard.
3. Excessive kindness or unfair partiality; preferential treatment.
4. A gift bestowed as a token of goodwill, kind regard, love, etc.[3]

Without a doubt, Mary must have been something special—*but she couldn't have been without sin.*

Romans 3:23 states that *"...all people have sinned, they have all fallen short of God's glory."* Remember, through Adam sin entered the world and spread to all men, causing all to sin. There was only One who was not effected by the fall of Adam. *"We have a chief priest who is able to sympathize with our weaknesses. He was tempted in every way that we are, but He (alone) didn't sin"* (Hebrews 4:15).

So as lovely and chaste as Mary was, she couldn't have been sinless because this was only accomplished by our Savior. And this fact should encourage us because the Bible says despite everyone's proneness to sin, *"His **favor** is with all who have an undying love for our Lord Jesus Christ" (Ephesians 6:24).*

So what does this mean for us?

<u>Favor means acceptance</u>: *"To the praise of the glory of His grace, wherein He has made us accepted in the beloved" (Ephesians 1:6).*

<u>Favor means great respect and kindness</u>: *"When God our Savior made His kindness and love for humanity appear, He saved us, but not because of anything we had done to gain His approval. Instead, because of His mercy He saved us through the washing in which the Holy Spirit gives us new birth and renewal" (Titus 3:4-5).*[4]

<u>Favor means to be loved</u>: *"But God is rich in mercy because of His great love for us. We were dead*

> You can give without loving, but you can never love without giving.
> -Author Unknown

because of our failures, but He made us alive together with

Christ. (It is God's kindness that saved you.) God has brought us back to life together with Christ Jesus and has given us a position in heaven with Him" (Ephesians 2:4-6).[5]

Just as God looked upon Mary *favorably*, He looks upon you and I the same way. You might be tempted to say, "But Mary was a virgin. She didn't have the past like I had..." This may be true, but virginity is more than just being an unmarried, untouched woman; it is a state of purity, a state of holiness. And God's Word says, *"But you have been washed and made holy, and you have received God's approval in the name of the Lord Jesus Christ and in the Spirit of our God" (1 Corinthians 6:11).[6]*

So regardless of your past, you were made pure and holy and righteous in His sight the moment you confessed and believed upon Jesus Christ as your Savior. *"For if by the one man's offense death reigned through the one, much more those who **receive** abundance of grace and of the gift of righteousness will reign in life through the One, Jesus Christ. Therefore, as through one man's offense judgment came to all men, resulting in condemnation, even so through one Man's righteous act **the free gift*** *came to all men, resulting in justification of life" (Romans 5:17-18).*

It's hard to receive such grace (and favor)—especially in the form of a gift. But just as the Angel said to Mary, the Lord would say to us: *Don't be afraid (overwhelmed, worried, fearful, or condemned)... You have found favor (acceptance and great respect) with God. He is pleased with you and you are loved by Him.*

Oh Happy Day!

As an illustration, I want to share a story with you. In 2004, all 276 members of Oprah's studio audience experienced a surreal moment. Every person, whether related or not, received keys to a brand-new car.[7] This was an unheard of present for that many people at one time. Reporters said the place erupted as people yelled, cried, screamed, sat down in disbelief, or jumped for joy! They were in awe of the magnitude of the gift they had received. I'm sure in some form or another they said, "Oh happy day!"

Prior to this give-away, Oprah had instructed her staff to find those who were "deserving," meaning they had to find people who were in desperate need of a car. Her staff reported back that only 57 people were found which was far short of filling the entire studio. But regardless of this fact, Oprah agreed to go ahead with the give-away to the entire studio audience—whether they all met the requirements or not.

Colossians 1:12 says we should *give "...thanks to the Father who has **qualified** us to be partakers of the inheritance of the saints in the light."* To qualify for something means you must have or meet the proper or necessary characteristics or requirements first. Or we could say, you must *be deserving*. But concerning salvation and righteousness, you and I did not meet the qualifications (not even close!) so we had to be "qualified" by some other means.

Remember, God's desire was to restore mankind. Buried under the heavy weight of sin with no means to help ourselves, God, with great generosity, gave His Son to the world as the perfect offering... the perfect gift. *"For by the power of the eternal Spirit, Christ offered Himself to God as a perfect sacrifice for our sins. That is why He is the One who mediates the new covenant between God and people, so that all who are invited can receive the eternal inheritance God has promised to them. For Christ died to set them free from the penalty of the sins they had committed" (Hebrews 9:14b-15).*[8]

Deserving or not, those who were invited to Oprah's big give-away walked away with a brand-new car. ***How much more have we received in Christ?*** Notice the writer of Hebrews said, *"...so that all who were invited can receive..."*

Can you picture a studio audience who has just been told that under their chairs is a box holding the keys to forgiveness and eternal life? At the revelation they have been freed from the punishment of their sins, the place would erupt (wouldn't it?)! In disbelief, some might yell in exuberant joy, while others might simply weep at the thought. Others might sit down in awe of what they've received, attempting to understand it all, while still others might rejoice like winners after the greatest victory of all time.

Oh happy day! One translation says Christ *"...entered the Most Holy Place once for all, having obtained eternal redemption" (9:12).* Eternal redemption means permanent deliverance. And I like the wording *"once for all."* Jesus will not have to die a second time. He went to the cross *once.* And He did it for *all.*

Deserving or not, He *"qualified us to be partakers of the inheritance of the saints in the light."* He made us fit to receive and take part in everything God has for us. So forget the car. Forget the party favors. There is nothing that can compare to the gift of eternal redemption—*our gift of righteousness.* Nothing. In light of the revelation of this great gift, everything else fades in comparison.

Chapter Eight

Qualified & Convinced

To forgive is to set a prisoner free, and then discover the prisoner was you.
-Lewis B Smedes

I recently went to an amusement park with several friends and our children. When one of the braver kids realized you had to be a certain height to ride, he became nervous he wouldn't meet the standard. Thankfully, he was a couple of inches tall enough and it wasn't a problem, but have you ever seen a child walk up to an amusement ride only to discover they are short of the required height to get on? Even if they try to stretch and tippy-toe themselves a little higher, the standard is set and they are disqualified (for now).

In a similar way, the Bible says, *"For all have sinned and **fall short** of the glory of God" (Romans 3:23).* The New Living Translation says, *"For all have sinned; all fall short of God's glorious standard."* And it's not just a few—sin is universal. ALL have fallen short of the standard set for God's glory. But just like the child who grew an inch over the summer and didn't have a problem being tall enough on his next visit to the amusement park, we too, have been raised up.

The standard didn't change... we did.

Not Short of the Glory

In his letter to the Romans, the Apostle Paul explains how everyone must meet the standard—no matter who you are or what you've done *(Romans 3:21-24).* But the good news is, the standard is met through faith in Jesus Christ. God made it possible for all who believe to be declared not guilty or disqualified. This means you're not short of the glory any longer!

You and I have been justified by our faith in Jesus. *"Moreover whom He predestined, these He also called; whom He called, these He also justified; and whom He justified, these He also glorified" (Romans 8:30).* This passage isn't insinuating God has favorites. On the contrary, it is identifying how God made it possible for us to be raised up. *"God knew what He was doing from the very beginning. He decided from the outset to shape the lives of those who love Him along the same lines as the life of His Son. The Son stands first in the line of humanity He restored. We see the original and intended shape of our lives there in Him. After God made that decision of what His children should be like, He followed it up by calling people by name. After He called them by name, He set them on a solid basis with Himself. And then, after getting them established, He stayed with them to the end, gloriously completing what He had begun" (Romans 8:29-30).[1]*

Every person has fallen short. But God has provided a spiritual resurrection for those in Christ. *"Because of His great love with which He loved us, even when we were dead in trespasses, made us alive together in Christ (by grace you have been saved), and **raised us up** together, and made us sit together in the heavenly places in Christ Jesus" (Ephesians 2:4-6).*

Earlier, I compared our "spiritual raising" to a child who grew over the summer in order to be qualified, but that's not an entirely accurate picture. In the natural, a child at the amusement park who found they were short of the height standard can only wait and *hope* they will grow taller in order to be qualified next time. But spiritually-speaking, when you gave your heart and life to Jesus through salvation, God *instantly* raised you up.

Although you were once disqualified from God's glory because of sin, your *faith* in Christ raised you to His standard! It's as if Jesus was the conductor at the amusement ride and when you approached Him and found yourself short of the standard, instead of rejecting and turning you away, Jesus picked you up and put you on His shoulders, *"...giving you joint seating with Him..."* [2]

Raised Up

"Sitting together in heavenly places in Christ Jesus" is not only referring to a future position in heaven; it also describes what you have now. Eternal life is not just a span of time in which you will live someday; it is also a *quality* of life that begins the moment you give your heart and life to Jesus Christ. You were *"raised with Him through faith in the working of God, who raised [Jesus] from the dead" (Colossians 2:12b).* This is present tense, not future tense.

The Bible doesn't say we will be raised... it says we were raised. *"And you, being dead in your trespasses and the uncircumcision of your flesh, He has made alive together with Him, having forgiven you all trespasses, having wiped out the handwriting of requirements that was against us, which was contrary to us. And He has taken it out of the way, having nailed it to the cross"* (Colossians 2:13-14).

Can you imagine the delight of the disqualified child who, when the conductor removed the measuring stick, was suddenly qualified by grace? The child knows it wasn't his or her own doing; it was by grace, and grace alone. They were short of the standard (the glory of God), yet the scripture says, *"Whoever believes on Him will not be put to shame"* (Romans 10:11). And this is true for every person—no matter who you are or what you've done.

> Nothing is more wretched than the mind of a man conscious of guilt.
>
> -Maccius Plautus

I was like that child... except I held my own measuring stick. Before I even approached, I mentally disqualified myself. But it was torturous to watch everyone else enjoy the ride, while I stood off to the side. So very timidly, little by little, I approached the throne of grace and was delighted when I discovered God had His own measuring stick and it was nothing like mine! *"But to each one of us grace was given according to the measure of Christ's gift" (Ephesians 4:7).* God didn't measure me according to my standard (good, bad, or ugly); He measured me according to Christ's gift.

The Requirement was Fulfilled

And that's not all. Paul said those who are in Christ Jesus, who walk (and live their lives) according to the Spirit, are not under the law of condemnation, for they have been raised up. *"For the law of the Spirit of life in Christ Jesus has made me free from the law of sin and death. For what the law could not do in that it was weak through the flesh, God did by sending His own Son in the likeness of sinful flesh, on account of sin: He condemned sin in the flesh, that the righteous requirement of the law might be fulfilled in us who do not walk according to the flesh but according to the Spirit" (Romans 8:2-4).*

God sent His Son Jesus to set us free from sin and death. On our own, you and I could never pay the price needed to be reconciled with God. But Jesus became our substitution and paid the penalty for our sins *"that the* **righteous requirement** *of the law might be fulfilled."* So what is the "righteous requirement" Paul is speaking of?

The answer is found in the same scripture we keep referring to: *"For He made Him who knew no sin to be sin for us, that we might become the RIGHTEOUSNESS of God in Him" (2 Corinthians 5:21).*

Righteousness is a big-sounding word but in Chapter Five, we learned it means to have right-standing with God. More specifically, it includes the ability to stand before Him without any guilt or inferiority as if you had never sinned.

But given this expanded definition, most Christians wouldn't say this describes their relationship with God. Most will agree we have a sin nature and we've all blown it. We're thankful for His forgiveness and we're thankful for our salvation and the promise to live eternally in Heaven, *but to daily feel like we can stand before God guilt-free?*... no way!

Yet the scripture clearly says, *"For He* (God) *made Him*

(Jesus) *who knew no* sin (who was perfect, who had never sinned) *to be sin for* us (who were not perfect and guilty of sin), *that we might* become (upon accepting Jesus as our Lord) *the righteousness of God in* Him (right-standing with God and the ability to stand before Him without any guilt or inferiority as if we had never sinned)" *(my paraphrase).*

This was the "righteous requirement" Paul was referring to in his letter to the Romans. This isn't my opinion—this is what the Bible says. So if Jesus paid the penalty for our sins so we could receive His righteousness, isn't it important for us to better understand what it is and how we received it?

Accounted for Righteousness

The first mention of righteousness is found in Genesis 15:5, when God made a promise to Abraham. He said, *"Look now toward heaven, and count the stars if you are able to number them. So shall your descendants be."* This was quite a promise. If you've ever studied the stars on a clear night, there are too many to count. Yet Abraham responded in faith. *"[Abraham] believed in the Lord, and*

[God] accounted it to him for righteousness" (verse 6).

At the time of this promise, Abraham had no children of his own, but God said his descendents would be as many as the stars in the sky. And without questioning why or how this could happen, *Abraham simply believed God.*

The New Testament describes this exchange between God and Abraham as a promise, or covenant. *"For when God made a promise to Abraham, because He could swear by no one greater, He swore by Himself, saying, 'Surely, blessing I will bless you and multiplying I will multiply you.' And so, after [Abraham] had patiently endured, he obtained the promise" (Hebrews 6:13-15).* By definition, a covenant or what the Bible refers to here as a promise, is a contract or agreement between two parties, whereas each party offers its best to the other.

But think about it: our God is perfect, for it is impossible for God to lie (Hebrews 6:18); whereas, Abraham was a mere man, like you and I, having faults and a sin nature. Therefore, how could God, being perfect, actually make covenant with an *imperfect* man? He couldn't. So He made a covenant with Himself on Abraham's behalf.

But that's not all. God, as the creator of the universe, had EVERYTHING to offer Abraham in this covenant. But what did Abraham have to give?

Look at Genesis 15 again: *"Then He brought him outside and said, 'Look now toward heaven, and count the stars if you are able to number them.' And He said to him, 'So shall your descendants be.' And [Abraham] **believed** in the Lord, and He accounted it to him for righteousness."* God could literally offer everything to Abraham, yet in exchange, all He wanted was to be believed.

The Bible says, *"[Abraham] did not waver at the promise of God through unbelief, but was strengthened in faith, giving glory to God, and being fully convinced that what He had promised He was also able to perform. And therefore 'it was accounted to him for righteousness'"* (Romans 4:20-22).

In other words, Abraham didn't waver at God's promise to make his descendents as many as the stars of the sky. He didn't question how God was going to do it. Instead he praised God and, through his praise, was strengthened in faith and therefore became "fully convinced" God was able to perform what He had promised.

And that's a good challenge for you and I. When we look into God's Word and see His promises, are we fully convinced they apply to us? Or do we believe they apply only to others?

When You Believed

A common problem among Christians is they're not "fully convinced" of what God's Word says because it doesn't line up with the way they think about or see themselves. Abraham could have easily done the same thing. He was close to one hundred years old and had no children of his own when God made him this promise. But Abraham decided not to look at his circumstances but instead believed God. It was at this point the Bible says God accounted it to him for RIGHTEOUSNESS.

Remember, righteousness is right-standing with God, including the ability to stand before Him without guilt or inferiority as if you had never sinned. God declared Abraham righteous *simply because he believed Him*.

This is all God asked of Abraham and it is all He ever

asks of us.

In Isaiah 42:6, speaking of Jesus, God said, *"I, the Lord, have called You to demonstrate my righteousness. I will guard and support You, for I have given You to My people as the personal confirmation of My covenant with them. And You will be a light to guide all nations to Me."* [1] Similar to the covenant God made with Abraham, God established a new covenant through His Son Jesus with us.

His part of the covenant is salvation and eternal life. Our part of the covenant is to believe on Him for the forgiveness of sins. To be born-again, we have to believe God and His promise of salvation. And just like Abraham believed and it was accounted to him for righteousness, when we believe God and accept Jesus as our Savior, it is accounted to us for righteousness also. This means you and I, at the moment of salvation, are given right-standing with God, the ability to stand before Him without any guilt or inferiority as if we had never sinned!

It doesn't matter if you've been born-again 15 years, 53

years, or 3 months, your righteousness began the moment you believed and accepted Jesus as your Savior.

Let me prove this to you.

To receive salvation, you had to confess and believe. The Bible says, *"If you confess with your mouth the Lord Jesus and believe in your heart that God has raised Him from the dead, you will be saved" (Romans 10:9).* But upon believing, God gives us so much more than just a ticket to Heaven. Romans 10:10 continues speaking of salvation: *"For with the heart **one believes unto righteousness,** and with the mouth confession is made unto salvation."*

Just like Abraham *"believed in the Lord, and He accounted it to him for righteousness,"* when we confess Jesus as our Lord and believe that God raised Him from the dead, it is also accounted to us, *"for with the heart one BELIEVES UNTO RIGHTEOUSNESS."* If Jesus took care of the sin, then upon believing, we are given His righteousness!

And this takes place at the moment of salvation—the very moment we believe.

You've Been Justified

Let's look again at Paul's account of Abraham. He said, *"And therefore 'it was accounted to [Abraham] for righteousness.' Now it was not written for his sake alone that it was imputed to him, but also for us. It shall be imputed to us who believe in Him who raised up Jesus our Lord from the dead, who was delivered up because of our offenses, and was raised because of our justification"* (Romans 4:22-25).

The Apostle Paul is speaking of righteousness. In other words, the story of Abraham, and how he received right-standing with God, was not written so we could put him on a pedestal and marvel at his faith. It was written so we would understand the same righteousness shall be imputed (meaning imparted or given) to us who believe also.

But notice how the above scripture states righteousness shall be given to those who believe in God who raised Jesus from the dead because of our "justification." Here's another big-sounding word that is very important.

Justification is God's declaration that the believing sinner is righteous and acceptable before Him.[2]

But hold on... can you be a "believing" sinner? These two words together almost sound like an oxymoron, yet the answer is yes—you can be a "believing sinner"—but only for one moment in time.

What God is calling a "believing sinner" is just that. It is a sinner (someone who has not yet believed in Jesus) that *now* believes. It is a very accurate picture of what takes place at salvation: We were sinners, who had no righteousness, and upon receiving Jesus as our Savior, we became believers with righteousness. Therefore, at the very moment we asked Jesus in our heart, there was a transformation which took place where, on our way to becoming a believer, we were a sinner first, thus making us for one moment in time a "BELIEVING SINNER."

And it was at that moment when justification took place, making the new believer righteous and acceptable before God. And that's when the title changes.

As soon as you accept Jesus as your Savior, you are no longer a *believing* sinner. You are now the righteousness of God in Christ—regardless of how you feel about it. And I know you may be thinking, can I say that? Can I really say I'm the righteousness of God in Christ? Yes. God's Word said it first.

We struggle with this thought because we're aware of our faults and failures, and it seems prideful and wrong to apply something to ourselves that befits Jesus more than us. But let me ask you this: Is it okay to say Jesus took our sin? We don't see Him as a sinner, but the fact remains He became something He was not.

And according to 2 Corinthians 5:21, just as God *made* Jesus become sin, He has *made* you righteous—something you were not, but now are in Him.

Chapter Nine

Misunderstood Revelation

What use is revelation or religion if it doesn't change anything?
-Bakir Bashir

Do you recall the story of Daniel and his experience in the lion's den?[1] It all started because Daniel was a righteous man who prayed night and day to his God. As an advisor to King Darius, he found favor with the king, making the other advisors jealous. These other men proposed an idea to King Darius to build a monument in his image and decree that all people should bow down and worship it in honor of him. They also proposed that all who would not bow down be thrown into the lion's den.

Can't He Change His Mind?

The idea pleased the king so he made the declaration. Later, after Daniel was accused of not bowing down to the idol because of his love and commitment to God, the king's decree demanded he be thrown to the lions. But King Darius loved Daniel very much. You would think that he, being the king, could change his mind and save Daniel from this awful punishment—but he could not.

Once a decree has been made by the king, it cannot be changed.

In the same manner, our God is King and once He declares a believing sinner to be righteous and acceptable before Him, IT CANNOT BE CHANGED. This is why, although we wrestle with understanding God's acceptance of us in spite of our sins and shortcomings, our struggle doesn't change His view.

In the last chapter, we said justification is God's declaration that the believing sinner is righteous and acceptable before Him. Our God is a righteous Judge. This definition is a picture of how God stands up from His throne when he sees a sinner receiving Jesus as their Savior. And in that moment, God smiles and declares, *"That child is mine – righteous and acceptable before Me!"* And when God declares something, it is settled in Heaven.

God made Jesus, who knew no sin, to become sin so we could become righteous and acceptable before Him when we believe He raised His Son from the dead. But make sure you have a clear picture of what took place at salvation.

I am bothered by Christians who say, "Well, I'm just a sinner saved by grace." I used to have a similar mentality, but it's not what the Bible teaches. The Bible says, *"For by grace you have been saved through faith, and that not of yourselves; it is the gift of God, not of works, lest anyone should boast" (Ephesians 2:8-9).* Notice it says, *"by grace you have been saved,"* –not "you are a sinner saved by grace."

Yes, we were all once sinners, and yes, we have a sin nature, but the Bible defines sinners as those who are separated from God, those who have not yet accepted His plan of salvation. Therefore, you and I, who are born-again, are no longer called sinners. The Bible calls us "Righteous" and this is why the definition of justification is so important to understand.

It is God's declaration that the believing sinner is

righteous and acceptable before Him. In that one moment in time, when you were a "believing sinner," it was then God declared you to be "righteous and acceptable before Him." And because of God's declaration, we can now stand before Him without any guilt or inferiority as if we had never been a sinner in the first place.

On the day I finally understood this, I rejoiced! The truth was, when I was born-again, I was declared righteous. And the same is true for you! If you were born-again yesterday, God declared you righteous. If you were born-again 53 years ago, God declared you righteous 53 years ago! The Bible clearly says the believer is righteous and acceptable before God without any guilt as if he or she had never sinned. And this righteousness was given to us by God's declaration the moment we received Jesus as our Savior and were born-again.

However, many of us have journeyed on this Christian walk not feeling one bit righteous...

Beginner Basics

I remember the first time I was tempted to pick up the

unforgiveness and condemnation I had laid down in front of my mirror. It's not so much that I remember exactly what it was I had done to make me feel guilty, but more that I remember the struggle of being tempted to beat myself up again.

Philippians 1:6 says we can be *"confident of this very thing, that He who has begun a good work in you will complete it until the day of Jesus Christ."* In my moment of weakness and self-condemnation, the Holy Spirit reminded me, *"There is therefore now no condemnation for those who are in Christ Jesus."* I wasn't entirely sure what this phrase meant, but as I told you earlier, I began to quote it often nonetheless. And with each confession, my temptation to pick up what I had laid down was lessened.

I later realized a bigger problem was that I didn't recognize what the Holy

> *The spiritual is parent of the practical.*
> -Thomas Carlyle

Spirit said to me *as scripture from the Bible!* I was certainly a babe in Christ.

And this is a problem with many Christians, even those

who have been born-again for years. They might recognize a scripture from the Bible, but they couldn't tell you where it's from, quote it on their own, or much less explain it. Paul said in Hebrews 5:12, *"You have been Christians a long time now, and you ought to be teaching others. Instead, you need someone to teach you again the basic things a beginner must learn about the Scriptures."* [2]

E.W. Kenyon once said, "All believers are in Christ, but [unfortunately] His Word is not in all believers." [3] This is sad, but true. The beginner basics found in God's Word, such as discovering God loves us and has forgiven *all* our sins, discovering (and understanding) how we've been made new creatures in Christ, and realizing when we make a mistake, there's *"no condemnation for those who are in Christ Jesus"* are the foundations of victorious living for every Christian.

However, if we don't learn these principles in God's Word and begin to renew our minds accordingly, we not only remain in the *beginner stage* permanently, but we are also perfect prey for the enemy.

It's a true statement that if we continue doing what we

have always done, we will continue having what we've always had. For instance, I was guilty of condemning myself. Although every mistake, every failure, and every ungodly thing I had committed in my past was forgiven by God the moment I was born-again, I continued to condemn myself for not knowing better. Ephesians 1:7 says, *"In Him we have redemption through His blood, the forgiveness of sins, according to the riches of His grace."* This grace was hard to accept. And in addition, I struggled with the good news that every mistake and failure made *after* accepting Jesus as my Savior was also forgiven each time I went to God and confessed my sins.

You are Forgiven

1 John 1:9 is a scripture you should never forget! It says, *"If we confess our sins, He is faithful and just to forgive us our sins and cleanse us of all unrighteousness."* This is a promise to born-again believers. Every time our heart is pierced with recognition of sin and our lips whisper, "I'm sorry God..." He is faithful to forgive our sin and wash it from His sight.

However, God's *"people are destroyed for a lack of knowledge" (Hosea 4:6a).* If we don't know God's Word says we are forgiven when we confess, then it is only natural to pick up the ugly feelings of guilt and condemnation... *again.*

Revelation of Right and Wrong

Knowledge can make us or break us. Because I didn't begin learning God's Word until I was already an adult (and had by that time committed more sins than I cared to count), my knowledge of sin tipped the scales in the wrong direction. I believed it was my past sins that kept me from having a closer relationship with God, so I was quite surprised to discover the great Apostle Paul was tempted to feel the same way.

He said, *"I felt fine when I did not understand what the law demanded. But when I learned the truth, I realized I had broken the law and was a sinner, doomed to die. So the good law, which was supposed to show me the way of life, instead gave me the death penalty" (Romans 7:9-10).*[4] Like myself, he struggled with the knowledge of sin mixed with his understanding of God's commandments.

I think we can all relate. Once we are born-again, our eyes are opened to a huge revelation of *right* and *wrong* that we didn't fully understand previously (if at all). Before we began hearing God's Word and it's commandments of do's and don'ts, we were fine. But, as Paul said, when we found out what we were supposed to be doing, and God's definition of sin, instead of bringing life or freedom, we found death.

Death is defined as separation from God, so in this case, Paul is referring to anything that separates us— including guilt and condemnation.

"So the good law, which was supposed to show me the way of life, instead gave me the death penalty. Sin took advantage of the law and fooled me; it took the good law and used it to make me guilty of death. But still, the law itself is holy and right and good. But how can that be? Did the law, which is good, cause my doom? Of course not! Sin used what was good to bring about my condemnation. So we can see how terrible sin really is. It uses God's good commandment for its own evil purposes" (Romans 7:10-13).[5]

Shame and guilt are never God's intention for the believer.

Revelation of God's Word, however, is intended to bring recognition of sin to our minds so we can turn from it. But our enemy, the devil, twists new revelation of right and wrong with the memory of our past, thus making our sin appear *"exceedingly sinful"* in our own mind. This then has opportunity to heap piles of guilt and condemnation on our shoulders, unnecessarily.

Condemnation vs. Conviction

One thing we all need to understand, though, is that the automatic result of sin *is* condemnation. In Romans 5:18, Paul said *"Yes, Adam's one sin brought condemnation upon everyone..."* In other words, through Adam's disobedience to God, judgment (and condemnation) came to all men. This judgment was an inherited sin nature that separated us from God. But God's plan was for reconciliation, not condemnation.

Satan brought sin into this world and condemnation is part of his package. God's desire is to have all mankind reconciled back to Him and to have close fellowship with His children. But without a clear revelation of reconciliation—in other words, what the believer has received from God at salvation—the feeling of condemnation that comes from sin is apt to stay.

After we are born-again, the Holy Spirit begins to deal with us regarding sin in the form of "conviction." Conviction is generally a gentle pull on the inside tugging us to make changes and adjustments in our life. Condemnation, on the other hand, is an ugly, harsh voice (not from God) that causes us to feel like a failure when we recognize sin in our life. And it's a continual battle for believers who have no knowledge of who they are in Christ to get out of this cycle of condemnation.

The problem is we try to fit into the mold of a "good Christian," yet inevitably fail because of sin. Condemnation then creeps in, attempting to keep us defeated. We may get victory over it for a while, but it isn't long before we are tempted to pick it back up, believing that little devil on our shoulder who keeps reminding us of our failures.

Naturally Speaking

The Bible says, *"The natural man does not receive the things of the Spirit of God, for they are foolishness to him;*

nor can he know them, because they are spiritually discerned (1 Corinthians 2:14). Upon accepting Jesus as our Savior, we are given a new nature. This new nature is found within us. Our hair and skin color or features don't change because these are all part of our outward man. When Paul said, *"If anyone is in Christ, he is a new creation; old things have passed away; behold, all things have become new" (2 Corinthians 5:17),* he was referring to the awakening of our spirit that now bears witness with God's Spirit.

The natural man is part of the "old" that passed away. In other words, whereas before salvation our natural man ruled everything, now after salvation, the natural man has a new Master—our spirit that bears witness with God's Spirit. The problem however, is that part of the natural man is his or her "mind, will and emotions" which are not automatically renewed to the things of God.

This area must be transformed day by day, from faith to faith, with continual feeding and monitoring. This is the reason our minds are attacked so often by the enemy. He plants suggestive thoughts, which seem to make sense to our "natural" mind, but remember, the *"natural man does not receive the things of the Spirit of God..."*

If we continue to depend *only* on our natural man, then we are destined to fail at the get-go. Why? Because *"...the things of God... are foolishness to [the natural man]..."* and the devil loves to take advantage of this fact.

For the most part, a large majority of the Body of Christ is a "sense knowledge" group of people who lean more on their understanding and how they feel than their ability to discern the things of the Spirit. This is why it is so easy for the devil to put condemnation on believers. It makes *sense* that we should feel guilty for our sins. And we should... But the problem is we have failed to train our spirits to discern and correctly evaluate our surroundings and circumstances based on God's Word.

Hebrews says, *"For everyone who partakes only of milk is unskilled in the **word of righteousness**, for he is a babe. But solid food belongs to those who are of full age, that is, those who by reason of use have their senses exercised to discern both good and evil" (Hebrews 5:13-14).*

This is interesting. Believers receive a new nature upon salvation, but that nature is a *baby*, regardless of how old the natural man or woman is.

To be full grown and "skilled" in righteousness, the believer has to *"by reason of use"* exercise their senses to discern what is of God and what is not. (A good example is: condemnation versus conviction.) In the natural, children learn by reason of "use" as they experiment and grow, no matter how many times they fail along the way. This principal is the same for spiritual things. Having a revelation of right and wrong, and then discerning correctly between condemnation and conviction completely dictates the rate of our growth in Christ.

Paul told Timothy, *"Be diligent to present yourself approved to God, a worker who does not need to be ashamed, rightly dividing the word of truth" (2 Timothy 2:15).* The King James Version says, *"Study to show thyself approved..."*

In other words, this aspect of our walk with God is vital to our growth because although we can be sincere, we can also be sincerely wrong. However, *"by reason of use"* we can correctly analyze the word of truth against our senses (how we feel or what we think about ourselves).

When we *"lean not on our own understanding, but in all our ways acknowledge God" (Proverbs 3:5-6)* and *"His way of doing things" (Matthew 6:33)*, we are actually learning to discern correctly. Therefore, *"The [NEW MAN* **can***] receive the things of the Spirit of God, for they are [NOT] foolishness to him; he [CAN] know them, because they are spiritually discerned (1 Corinthians 2:14, my paraphrase).*

As I began to study God's Word and pursue His truth, I finally found the scripture the Holy Spirit always prompted me to say each time I was tempted to hold on to my guilt: *"There is therefore now no condemnation for those who are in Christ Jesus."* Ironically, it was written by the Apostle Paul in Romans 8:1, right after he confessed having his own struggle with the same.

Chapter Ten

Resisting Condemnation

Compassion will cure more sins than condemnation.
-Henry Ward Beecher

A friend of mine was recently feeling a bit condemned because she had struggled with thoughts of quitting something that was in her best interest. She hadn't quit, but was still mad at herself for even entertaining the thoughts. I reminded her that she was a three-part being.

In 1 Thessalonians 4:17, the Bible says we are *"...spirit, soul, and body..."* The body is the house where our spirit and soul reside. The spirit is the part of us which is born-again and in contact with God; and the soul is the realm of our mind, will and emotions. She was feeling guilty over the thought of quitting, when in reality, those thoughts were simply the conversation between her *soul* and *spirit*. I enthusiastically reminded her that her spirit had won because she hadn't quit.

The Apostle Paul said, *"I say then: Walk in the Spirit, and you shall not fulfill the lust of the flesh. For the flesh lusts against the Spirit, and the Spirit against the flesh; and these are contrary to one another, so that you do not do the things that you wish" (Galatians 5:16-17).* In other words, when the flesh (or we could say, our soul) is in spiritual warfare with our spirit (the part of us that belongs to God), one or the other is going to win—but not both.

Dominant Identity

I guess we could compare it to being pregnant with fraternal twins. Inside of every believer, there are two identities and they are completely opposite of one another. It would help us to picture these two constantly fighting and warring with each another until one finally submits.

Over time, the one which is strongest will become dominant while the weaker one becomes compliant and even docile. The word "docile" simply means something that is readily trained or taught. If the spirit of a man becomes the dominant identity, this is good. This means the flesh nature of the man has become compliant and even readily trained to submit.

However, if these are reversed and the flesh, or soul, is the dominant identity, this can be bad. Instead of being spirit-led, this person is controlled by their mind, will, and emotions. It's the reason Paul said, *"For what I am doing, I do not understand. For what I will to do, that I do not practice; but what I hate, that I do" (Romans 7:15).*

The very emotions and decisions made by the flesh are like a boomerang that turns on you, and what felt good at the moment, is now the culprit of guilt and condemnation. Why? Because the flesh lusts against the spirit and the two are contrary to one another.

People often wonder, "Well, how will I know if I'm in the flesh or in the spirit?" The Bible gives us a full-proof test. Galatians 5:22-23 says, *"Now the fruit of the Spirit is love, joy, peace, longsuffering, kindness, goodness, faithfulness, gentleness, and self-control."* If a person can recognize these in operation in their life, this is then proof of being led by their spirit. However, if there is a *lack* of these, this is proof of being led by the flesh.

And of all the fruits of the spirit, *self-control* is the one we must pay attention to the most because all the others will be in check if we keep a tab on this one. Self-control simply means you are allowing the *real you on the inside* to call all the shots. We could call it "spirit-controlled." In other words, when our mind, will, and emotions are fighting us, the battle will be won when we allow our spirit to have the last word.

The problem is that just like twins in a mother's womb must be fed through the umbilical cord, the flesh and the spirit are hungry also. Whichever one we choose to feed the most will be the stronger of the two.

People are often discouraged because when they want to do good they can't seem to. In those cases, it would be good to ask, "What have you been feeding your spirit lately?" My friend was frustrated with the fight within her. But what she didn't realize was she must have been feeding her spirit because her flesh didn't win. Yet, in her limited knowledge, she entertained condemnation unnecessarily nonetheless.

The Bible says when sin entered the world through

Adam and Eve, judgment came to all men from that point forward. *"Therefore, as through one man's offense judgment came to all men, resulting in condemnation, even so through one Man's righteous act the free gift came to all men, resulting in justification of life"* (Romans 5:18). In other words, we're all born with a sin nature, which automatically produces condemnation. But after salvation, any struggle the believer has with condemnation is *never* from God.

(I repeat... never.)

> *Guilt is perhaps the most painful companion to death.*
> -Coco Chanel

God's correction always comes through conviction—not condemnation. *"There is therefore now no condemnation for those who are in Christ Jesus"* (Romans 8:1). Condemnation is applied to the non-believer, while conviction is applied to the believer. John 3:18 says, *"He who believes in Him is not condemned; but he who does not believe is condemned already, because he has not believed in the Name of the only begotten Son of God."*

But remember, without a clear revelation of what the

believer received when he or she was born-again (forgiveness and right-standing with God), condemnation is apt to stay. In other words, the devil will convince you it is natural to feel condemned for sin, because in his words "we are guilty and unworthy." And this is true—partially. Let me ask you this question: Are you born-again? If yes, then you are *"in Christ Jesus"* and the Bible says, *"There is no condemnation <u>for those who are in Christ Jesus</u> who do not walk according to the flesh…"*

Our flesh is simply those *feelings* and *desires* that are governed by our mind, will, and emotions. Paul is stating there is no condemnation for those who do **not** walk, or live life, according to their feelings. So would the opposite be true? Yes, most definitely. There **is** a door for condemnation for those who live life always following their feelings.

I've told you before, I was guilty of condemning myself because I was governed every day by my own feelings of unworthiness and insecurity. Therefore, I lived under a huge cloud of condemnation all the time. I never felt I could do anything right. But God wasn't responsible for my wrong thinking—I made a choice to follow my feelings, which opened the door for condemnation from the devil.

Paul said, *"There is therefore now no condemnation for those who are in Christ Jesus, who do not walk according to the flesh, but according to the Spirit."* John 4:24 says, *"God is Spirit and those who worship Him must worship Him in spirit and in truth."* When the Apostle Paul said there is no condemnation for those who walk according to the "Spirit," he is referring to God. There is no condemnation to those who are walking according to God, or we could say, according to the *law* of God.

To break it down even further, we could say, there is no condemnation for those who are walking according to what God has said in His Word.

Baffled

Looking at Paul's life, we discover he had a strong revelation of who he was in Christ. In fact, inspired by the Holy Spirit, Paul wrote more of the New Testament than any other person. Yet, this same man confessed he struggled in the flesh. He had been given a new nature through salvation, but his fleshly desires were constantly at war with his *new* nature. It's a struggle we can identify with—from the moment we wake up each day until we go to bed each night, our new nature battles with the desires of our flesh, or our feelings.

And if our minds aren't renewed in God's Word regarding our right-standing with Him, we will naturally allow our feelings to override God's Word. Paul said he was baffled because he couldn't' seem to practice or accomplish what he wished, but instead did the things he actually loathed (and later felt guilty for). He also admitted he was tempted to believe his feelings. He said, *"O wretched man that I am! Who will deliver me from this body of death?" (Romans 7:24).*

Does that sound familiar? Have your feelings ever said something similar?

"I'm pitiful."

"I don't know why I try."

"I can't do anything right."

Like Paul, often that's how we want to *feel*, but it's not

the truth. And Paul knew this too. He admitted his feelings, but then immediately made a choice not to follow how he felt because he knew it was contrary to God's Word. He said *"O wretched man that I am! Who will deliver me from this body of death? I thank God— through Jesus Christ our Lord! So then, with the **mind** I myself serve the law of God, but with the **flesh** the law of sin"* (Romans 7:24-25). Paul fully realized his flesh, or feelings, would always choose the law of sin. But *"with (his) mind"* he could make a choice to serve the law of God (consciously deciding to follow what God said about him instead of what his feelings were telling him).

Paul said, *"I was alive once without the law, but when the commandment came, sin revived and I died. And the commandment, which was to bring life, I found to bring death"* (Romans 7:9-10). He wasn't talking about literal death here. He was describing how he felt regarding the conflict between his flesh and his new nature in Christ.

In other words, the Word that was supposed to bring him life, or freedom, he found to bring death, or condemnation. His understanding of sin left him feeling guilty. But God, through the Holy Spirit, enlightened his understanding regarding the difference between following after the flesh and following after the Spirit. *"For those who live according to the flesh set their minds on the things of the flesh, but those who live according to the Spirit, the things of the Spirit. For to be carnally minded is **death**, but to be spiritually minded is **life and peace**"* (Romans 8:5-6).

In other words, those who constantly think and meditate on their feelings (or flesh) will live according to, or we could say "dominated by," those feelings. The Amplified Bible describes the "death" which arises from being carnally minded as being that which *"...comprises all the miseries arising from sin."* For example, if our feelings are filled with guilt, condemnation, low self-esteem or unworthiness, then we will *live* in relation to those miserable feelings.

On the other hand, if we'll begin to meditate and (constantly) think on what God's Word says about us and who we are in Christ, then our feelings will work in the positive instead of the negative. We have the promise of life and peace if we will just set our minds on the things of the Spirit. But if we decide to believe and trust only in our feelings, then we will live our entire life according to those feelings, never finding true peace. To be "carnally minded" simply means our sinful nature is in control. And according to God's Word, the only thing that can come from a "carnal" mindset is death, or condemnation.

Faith & Feelings

In the eyes of God, when I confessed Jesus as my Lord and Savior, I was a new creation endowed with righteousness. However, my feelings about myself dictated otherwise, and so, I let my feelings decide.

We need to understand that righteousness is never based on our feelings.

God's Word never changes. However, our feelings change constantly, depending on our circumstances. Therefore, if our faith is in our feelings, which do change, then our faith will imitate our feelings by constantly changing. But if our faith is in God's Word, which never changes, then our faith won't waver, regardless of our circumstances or our feelings.

The good news is that those who make a decision to

believe and trust in the Word of God—regardless of what their feelings say—will live according to the Spirit in abundant *life* and *peace*, for *"there is therefore now no condemnation for those who are in Christ Jesus, who do not walk according to the flesh, but according to the Spirit."*

So in our attempt to reflect Christ as best as possible, it is important that our spirits become more in tune with God's Word. Righteousness is first a position we've been given in Christ, and then the actions which follow. This includes resisting condemnation, and moving forward after repentance.

Chapter Eleven

Engrafted

A man finds his identity by identifying.
-Author Unknown

Like every little girl, when I was growing up, I had a "BFF"—*a best friend forever*. Her name was Tori and she and I were about the same height and weight, and we both had blonde hair. It didn't matter if we were with her mom, or my mom, people would always ask if we were twins. But I realize now, it had little to do with our physical similarities. We spent so much time together as young girls that we actually began to *act* like one another. Our mannerisms were the same and we could finish each other's sentences because we also *thought* the same.

Becoming Like Him

The Bible says, *"For He made Him who knew no sin to be sin for us that we might become the righteousness of God in Him" (2 Corinthians 5:21).* In other words, there was a great exchange. Jesus took our sin (becoming sin for us) and we took His righteousness (becoming like Him).

Another aspect of our new life in Christ involves being "engrafted" in Him. In horticulture, the word engrafted refers to a cut made in the stem of a plant whereas another plant-life with an identical cut is placed in the slot so the two combine and grow as one. This is generally only successful between two *closely related* species.

The Book of James says, *"...receive with meekness the **engrafted** word, which is able to save your souls" (1:21).* As I've already mentioned, the soul of a person is their mind, will and emotions. Before receiving Christ, our soul leans toward sinful tendencies. After salvation however, our soul is constantly in the process of being renewed to the image and nature of Christ. Therefore, God's Word is vital when it comes to rescuing our soul (our mind, will and emotions) from danger, possible harm, injury or loss.

This alone, is enough reason to cling to God's Word—it saves us *from us.*

So consider the word engrafted and think again about its meaning. It describes a cut made in one species so another closely related species can be placed in the cut, blend and grow with the dominant source, thus resulting in one new creation. James said God's Word is engrafted into those who will receive it, but this is not always an easy, or painless, task. *"For the word of God is living and powerful, and sharper than any two-edged sword,* **piercing** *even to the division of soul and spirit, and of joints and marrow, and is a discerner of the thoughts and intents of the heart" (Hebrews 4:12).*

In essence, the word engrafted describes being "wounded." God's Word has been known to step on toes and address areas we'd rather leave undisturbed. But remember, the goal is to *save* and *rescue* us from our own mind, will, and emotions, which are a constant playground for Satan.

The Psalmist said, *"O God... deal with me for Your name's sake... I am poor and needy, and my heart is wounded within me" (Psalm 109:21-22).* In his prayer, he specifically asked God to check him. Then he said his heart (the part of us with which God deals) was wounded within him.

When we acknowledge our need and make ourselves vulnerable to God by being honest and open with Him, His Word then inserts itself in the wound (of our brokenness), binding itself to our heart to add life and bring growth. This is really amazing because successful engrafting can only take place between two *closely related* species. Remember, Christians are new creations *in* Christ Jesus. As such, we have taken on His nature, becoming like Him.

But that's not all! Using horticulture as our example again, when a plant is engrafted into another, it is very common for one plant to sprout and produce the blooms of the other species on its own stems. As a Christian, you are called to produce *"fruits of righteousness" (Philippians 1:11).* In other words, as you allow His Word to address and remove your shame, guilt, and pain, the wound these areas leave behind soon become a branch overflowing with the blooms of God's nature.

This is what I tried to explain to Benjamin as a young boy already tempted to dislike who he was. He was made in the image of God, and so was my friend who struggled with homosexuality. Despite how either of them felt, their faith in Christ and understanding of God's Word, *mixed with time*, would reveal His nature in them eventually.

> *Forgiveness is the fragrance that the flower leaves on the heel of the one who crushed it.*
> -Author Unknown

And there's one more important fact we need to understand about the engrafting process: **Jesus was wounded first.** The prophet Isaiah said, *"Surely He has borne our griefs and carried our sorrows; yet we esteemed Him stricken, smitten by God, and afflicted. But He was **wounded** for our transgressions, He was bruised for our iniquities; the chastisement for our peace was upon Him, and by His stripes we are healed"* (Isaiah 53:4-5).

Remember, this was God's plan. When Jesus took our sins, a spiritual cut was made which allowed us to be placed *in Him.* If He had not been wounded, there would have been no cut and no place for us to be grafted in. Yet now, because He fulfilled the righteous requirement, we have the privilege of allowing His nature to overtake our nature so others will see Him in us.

Renewing our Minds

The reason these truths are sometimes hard to accept is because we have given more weight to the world's way of doing things than God's way. Paul said in Romans 12:2, *"Do not be conformed to this world, but be transformed by the renewing of your mind that you may prove what is that good and acceptable and perfect will of God."* For example, God's forgiveness of our sins when we give our life to Jesus transforms how He sees us. He no longer sees the sins we've committed. But we often continue seeing ourselves the same way we did before we were born-again—through the eyes of guilt, condemnation, and comparison—because our minds have not yet been renewed to God's Word.

After I received salvation, I continued to struggle with insecurities and fears in my attempts to fit into a new mold, desperately wanting to be accepted by God and others. But in God's eyes, I was already a new creature in Christ. I just couldn't see it because my mind had not yet been renewed to these truths. Therefore, I carried all the same mentalities and struggles I had had in the world into my walk with Christ, only this time, I tried to conform them into a new package—that of *a Christian*.

And the majority of the time, this is true of most new believers who don't know how he or she measures up in God's eyes. Sometimes they attempt to figure it out by observing other believers, but sadly, that's not a full-proof plan because others may be just as lost when it comes to their identity in Christ.

The best place to discover who you are in Christ is by His example and as described in His Word.

For instance, in most cases, when we received salvation (engrafted into Him), faith was originally birthed in our heart based on the message of God's grace, love, and forgiveness. Yet because we know what we've done and what God is actually offering to forgive, we struggle with these truths. But God's Word encourages us to believe it regardless of how we *feel* or what we *think* true justice should look like.

Forgiven

Are you familiar with the Bible story of the woman

caught in adultery? You and I may or may not have ever been in shoes like hers, but nonetheless, in our own mind, our sin is just as hard to bear. So despite her obvious guilt (and ours), let's look at this story not just as a picture of initial salvation, but instead as a true depiction of God's continuing love, understanding, and instruction:

Early in the morning (at dawn), He came back into the temple [court], and the people came to Him in crowds. He sat down and was teaching them when the scribes and Pharisees brought a woman who had been caught in adultery. They made her stand in the middle of the court and put the case before Him. "Teacher," they said, "This woman has been caught in the very act of adultery. Now Moses in the Law commanded us that such [women—offenders] shall be stoned to death. But what do You say [to do with her—what is Your sentence]?"

This they said to try (and test) Him, hoping they might find a charge on which to accuse Him.

But Jesus stooped down and wrote on the ground with

His finger. However, when they persisted with their question, He raised Himself up and said, "Let him who is without sin among you be the first to throw a stone at her." Then He bent down and went on writing on the ground with His finger. They listened to Him, and then they began going out, conscience-stricken, one by one, from the oldest down to the last one of them, till Jesus was left alone, with the woman standing there before Him in the center of the court.

When Jesus raised Himself up, He said to her, "Woman, where are your accusers? Has no man condemned you?" She answered, "No one, Lord." And Jesus said, "I do not condemn you either. Go on your way and from now on sin no more" (John 8:2-11).[1]

Did you hear Him correctly?

Do you realize this is still what the Lord is saying today? *"Go and sin no more."*

When the devil, our own conscience, or anyone else, brings an accusation against us, do you realize God's first reaction to us is the same as Jesus had with this woman? *"Go and sin no more."* She was guilty but Jesus showed compassion. He didn't condone her sin by understanding it; He simply revealed the nature and heart of God by not condemning her.

Many theologians believe when Jesus was writing in the dirt with his finger that He was identifying the sins of those in the crowd. As their conscience was pricked, they left one by one. Because the truth is, when we find ourselves guilty of sin, we should be bruised with sorrow over it. In other words, just because God offers grace doesn't mean we should take it lightly.

But at the same time, we need to understand the heart of God is compassionate (and holy) and His desire is to teach us, because unfortunately we will fail again. But He also knows we have been engrafted with His nature, and patience is required. The *fruit of righteousness* will show up eventually.

What Jesus said to the woman is what He is still saying to us today, *"Go and sin no more."* This is our instruction. It means, "Learn your lesson. Receive forgiveness. Don't do it again."

Many times I have had to go to God in prayer and

express my sincere remorse for failing again at something I felt I knew better. Failing again for the same thing didn't necessarily mean I was taking forgiveness for granted. On the contrary, it meant I was growing. The danger would be if I committed the same sin again (and again) but I *wasn't* grieved by it. Just as a child learning to walk, stumbles and picks themselves back up only to stumble again as their legs grow stronger, we sometimes fail because our spiritual legs are weak too.

God understands this and it is why He says again (and again), *"Go and sin no more."*

Our response should be, "Yes, Lord." And then our actions should match our words. When sin is revealed in our lives, we should repent. The word repent is defined in the Greek as meaning *to think differently*. Therefore, repentance isn't just an action—it's also a mental decision.

It insinuates we must first recognize the wrong in our life before we can change it. The Apostle Paul said, *"Don't copy the behavior and customs of this world, but let God transform you into a new person by changing the way you think.* *Then you will learn to know God's will for you, which is good and pleasing and perfect"* (Romans 12:2).[2]

We can't change our past. But despite the remorse, guilt, and temptations of our flesh, we can be changed. *"For we have the mind of Christ"* *(1 Corinthians 2:16b),* and therefore, we are infused with His nature and His righteousness.

Chapter Twelve

Performance Not Required

The wheel's spinning, but the hamster's dead.
-Author Unknown

When Benjamin was sixteen years old and had just gotten his driver's license, it was a little scary for me. But it was also fun to watch him grow up and become a man. One day his truck was giving him some trouble and seemed to be low on oil, so he began tinkering around on it in our front driveway. His dad was out of town, so there were several phone calls back and forth in an attempt to fix the problem, all while I was inside doing laundry.

More than Sweat

Some time later, Benjamin came in to say that he thought it was fixed and, "Oh by the way Mom, can you wash this shirt? I need it for athletics tomorrow." He proceeded to toss me a grey t-shirt, which I quickly added to a load I was just putting in the washer. Afterward, when the same load came out of the dryer, I pulled out the grey t-shirt to fold only to notice it had big stains all over it. About that time, Benjamin walked by and I asked if the school had given it to him like that. His response? "No, I used it to change my oil."

What?! Not only was this the wrong thing to use to check oil, but I had just thrown it into my washer thinking the only thing it carried was teenage sweat!

This incident reminds me of Isaiah 64:5, which says, *"But we are all like an unclean thing, and all our righteousnesses are like filthy rags."* And there are two ways to look at this scripture. First, there is nothing we can do to earn our right-standing with God. And secondly, once God has clothed us with His righteousness, we have a responsibility to keep it clean.

Let's look at earning our righteousness first. On our very best day, any good we've done is still a filthy rag in comparison to the price Jesus paid to cover our sins. The only way to receive righteousness is by faith and repentance. Romans 10:10 says, *"For with the heart one believes unto righteousness..."* And Paul said, *"Now to him who works, the wages are not counted as grace but as debt. But to him who does not work but believes on Him who justifies the ungodly, his faith is accounted for righteousness, just as David describes [the happiness of an undeserving sinner who is declared to be righteous] apart from works" (Romans 4:4-6).*

All believers receive right-standing with God the day they are born-again—the day they believed. So righteousness isn't something that is going to happen, nor is it something we are working towards or might be someday because of our performance. No. Righteousness was automatic the day we first believed in our heart and confessed Jesus as our Lord.

There's Not Enough Good Works

The Bible says Abraham is the father of our faith and he received righteousness because he believed God. So we need to understand he didn't earn it. His right-standing with God was through the righteousness of faith. *"For the promise that he would be the heir of the world was not to Abraham or to his seed through the law, but through the righteousness of faith" (Romans 4:13).*

The "law" refers to our works (or performance). Too many Christians have the mentality that good works will eventually make you righteous. They sincerely believe righteousness is something they are working toward. "Well, if I could just get my act together and quit messing up all the time, *then maybe someday* I'll be in right-standing with God."

Although it is important to live right and do our best not to sin, those things in and of themselves will not make you any more righteous than you already are.

Let me explain... I felt like I couldn't reach God because I was trapped in a box of unforgiveness and I had no knowledge of what Jesus had done for me or how God saw me through Him. I tried very hard to reach God through my "works" by fitting into a certain mold. Out of desperation, I started praying and asking for His help. I needed revelation. Just as I had worked hard in the world to "fit in," I was working very hard at being a "perfect" Christian, but was getting nowhere.

At one point, God encouraged me to be the best I knew how to be, and it was good and right for me to focus on those things. I needed to get my eyes off my problems and on to Him. But God already knew I'd be spinning my wheels. My works were dead, getting me nowhere, but I kept spinning that wheel anyway.

The funny thing is, God doesn't allow us to walk through things so HE can see of what we're made; He already knows. He allows us to walk through things so WE can see of what we're made. And I needed to see how my entire life had been built on works.

Righteousness is received by faith—not by the things we do (or don't do). Concerning Abraham, Paul said, *"What then shall we say that Abraham our father has found according to the flesh? For if Abraham was justified by works, he has something to boast about, but not before God. For what does the Scripture say? 'Abraham believed God, and it was accounted to him for righteousness.' Now to him who works, the wages are not counted as grace but as debt. But to him who does not work but believes on Him who justifies the ungodly, his faith is accounted for righteousness" (Romans 4:1-5).*

Basically, Paul was saying it was impossible for

Abraham's works to bring him righteousness—just like it is impossible for our *works* to bring us righteousness.

I like the way the New Living Translation reads these verses: *"Abraham was, humanly speaking, the founder of our Jewish nation. What were his experiences concerning this question of being saved by faith? Was it because of his good deeds that God accepted him? If so, he would have had something to boast about. But from God's point of view Abraham had no basis at all for pride. For the Scriptures tell us, 'Abraham believed God, so God declared him to be righteous.' When people work, their wages are not a gift.* **Workers earn what they receive.** *But people are declared righteous because of their faith, not because of their work."*

> My salvation was a free gift. I didn't have to work for it and it's better than any gold medal I've ever won.
>
> -Betty Cuthbert (4-time Olympic Champion)

Abraham believed God, that's it. And therefore, God gave him the gift of righteousness. It was nothing he could have earned through his works. And the same is still true for us today.

The Righteousness of Faith

What's interesting is that God's chosen people, Israel, had been given the promise of a Savior and yet when the Savior came, they didn't believe in Him. Instead, they believed they had to "earn" their righteousness through the things they did. But the Gentiles, who were not God's chosen people, actually attained righteousness (right-standing with God, including the ability to stand before Him without any guilt or inferiority as if they had never sinned) simply because they *believed*.

"What shall we say then? That Gentiles, who did not pursue righteousness, have attained righteousness, even the righteousness of faith; but Israel, pursuing the law of righteousness, has not attained to the law of righteousness. Why? Because they did not seek it by **faith***, but as it were, by the works of the law"* (Romans 9:30-32a).

How many Christians today are doing exactly the same thing?

I know in my ignorance, I tried to gain right-standing with God through the good things I did (in other words, I tried to earn it). But Paul said the promise was to Abraham and his seed through the righteousness of faith, not the law. There is nothing you or I could ever do to earn our righteousness. We must seek it by faith, meaning, we must believe.

But when we're ignorant of God's righteousness and seek to establish it on our own by the things we do instead of by faith, we've missed God's plan and forgotten our part of the covenant was always to BELIEVE.

Christ Didn't Die in Vain

Romans 10:3-4 says, *"For they, being ignorant of God's righteousness, and seeking to establish their own righteousness, have not submitted to the righteousness of God. For Christ is the end of the LAW of righteousness to everyone who believes."* Again, the "law of righteousness" refers to the things we do. But remember, if we could earn our righteousness, then it wouldn't have been necessary for God to send His Son as the final sacrifice for our sins.

But as it were, we were separated from God, with no

hope, and in desperate need of a Savior.

So it is by grace that we are saved. Ephesians 2:8-9 says, *"For by grace you have been saved through faith, and that not of yourselves, it is the gift of God, not of works, lest anyone should boast."* The key here is *"through faith"* we have been saved. If we could earn salvation through our performance then what was the point of Jesus' death and resurrection? **So why is righteousness any different?**

Don't forget that it is at salvation, the moment we believed in Jesus, that we received our right-standing with God in the first place. *"I do not set aside the grace of God; for if righteousness comes through the law, then Christ died in vain" (Galatians 2:21).*

We have got to get over our "works" mentality. The number of times we go to church, the number of times we follow God's commandments, (etc., etc.), is not going to increase our righteousness in God's eyes. His Word is established as a guideline for us to follow and it is always in our best interest. So we absolutely need to follow His commandments, but righteousness is not something we are working towards.

The bottom line is this: *"For no one can ever be made right in God's sight by doing what His law commands. For the more we know God's law, the clearer it becomes that we aren't obeying it. But now God has shown us a different way of being right in his sight—not by obeying the law but by the way promised in the Scriptures long ago. We are made right in God's sight when we trust in Jesus Christ to take away our sins. And we all can be saved in this same way, no matter who we are or what we have done. For all have sinned; all fall short of God's glorious standard. Yet now God in His gracious kindness declares us not guilty. He has done this through Christ Jesus, who has freed us by taking away our sins. For God sent Jesus to take the punishment for our sins and to satisfy God's anger against us. We are made right with God when we believe that Jesus shed his blood, sacrificing his life for us. God was being entirely fair and just when He did not punish those who sinned in former times. And He is entirely fair and just in this present time when He declares sinners to be right in His sight because they believe in Jesus"* (Romans 3:20-26).[1]

God has given us His righteousness based on our faith.

And the Bible says, *"I will greatly rejoice in the Lord, my soul shall be joyful in my God; for He has clothed me with the garments of salvation, He has covered me with the robe of righteousness..." (Isaiah 60:10).* God clothed us based on faith, not performance. But after the fact, it is true our righteousness *should produce* good works.

Keep it Clean

So referring to our attempts to earn salvation, Isaiah said, *"But we are all like an unclean thing, and all our righteousnesses are like filthy rags."* But what if you received salvation (and a robe of righteousness) by faith and then still tried to live like you used to? I'm afraid that is only going to produce a filthy rag.

My son had been given a brand-new t-shirt for athletics. He was instructed to wear it at practice every day, as an identification. After the oil change incident, he still had to wear the same shirt, but now it had permanent grease marks all over it. His shirt still identified him from non-athletes, but what representation did his shirt now display?

This may be a silly example, but do you see the parallel?

When God gives us right-standing with Himself and puts a robe of righteousness on us, we now represent our King. Our robe of righteousness sets us apart from non-believers. But if we're not careful, our robes can become filthy—through pride, works, sin, or even inferiority.

My own robe has been stained from poor judgment, flesh fits, and the like. Thankfully, God has a washing machine that cleanses from all unrighteousness! *"If we [freely] admit that we have sinned and confess our sins, He is faithful and just (true to His own nature and promises) and will forgive our sins [dismiss our lawlessness] and [continuously] cleanse us from all unrighteousness" (1 John 1:9).[2]*

This is a scripture we should quote, stand on, and depend on all the time! But listen to the instruction surrounding this promise: *"This is the message which we have heard from Him and declare to you, that God is light and in Him is no darkness at all. If we say that we have fellowship with Him, and walk in darkness, [we're not living what we claim.] But if we walk in the light as He is in the light, we have fellowship with one another, and the blood of Jesus Christ His Son cleanses us from all sin. If we say that we have no sin, we deceive ourselves, and the truth is not in us. If we confess our sins, He is faithful and just to forgive us our sins and to cleanse us from all unrighteousness. If we say that we have not sinned, we make Him a liar, and His word is not in us" (1 John 1:5-10).*

It is so important that we live what we claim. We must understand this is part of our righteousness as well. Otherwise, we make Him a liar and our robe of righteousness is nothing but a filthy rag. Remember, *"the kindness and the love of God our Savior toward man appeared, not by works of righteousness which we have done, but according to His mercy..." (Titus 3:4-5).* And because He saved us, we now represent Him everyday. We are symbols of His Kingdom. If we fail (and we do sometimes), then let us acknowledge it and give it to the only One who can cleanse us and put us back in right-standing with Himself.

God said, *"No weapon formed against you shall prosper, and every tongue which rises against you in judgment you shall condemn. This is the heritage of the Lord, **and their righteousness is from Me**, says the Lord" (Isaiah 54:17).*

Chapter Thirteen

Mirror, Mirror

There are two ways of spreading light: to be the candle or the mirror that reflects it.
-Edith Wharton

Mirror, Mirror, on the Wall
Who is really Lord of all?
Mirror, Mirror, on the Wall
Christ in me means hope for all.

This simple, yet powerfully truthful, poem was written by my dear friend, Marie Myers. She and I have traveled together and ministered in the United States and overseas to women of all backgrounds. She is one of those special people who sharpen me. We both have similar stories of coming to Christ as adults, so we share a zeal for what it means to be made the righteousness of God in Christ.

On one such trip, we sat in our hotel room like two schoolgirls having a slumber party, talking for hours about what Christ has done for us. As we shared, Marie said, "Some people's only hope of seeing Christ is through His reflection in us." In other words, God desires to reflect His glory through you and I, because the world isn't offering the right stuff.

2 Corinthians 3:18 says, *"But we all, with unveiled face, beholding as in a mirror the glory of the Lord, are being transformed into the same image from glory to glory, just as by the Spirit of the Lord."* Isn't it interesting that the Bible says we behold the glory of the Lord when we look in our mirrors? This was news to me... After giving my heart to Jesus, I can't say I saw anything which closely resembled Him, or His glory, when I looked in my mirror. But that was *my* perspective—not His.

To be "unveiled" means to take the mask off and truly reveal yourself. We know God can already see us (with or without a mask), so the instruction is directed more toward allowing others to see us. But not just *us*, meaning the fearful, insecure, or broken, but the *new* us—that which has been redeemed and repurposed for Christ. In other words, we need to allow others to see *Him* in us.

The Amplified Bible says, *"And all of us, as with unveiled face, [because we] continued to behold [in the Word of God] as in a mirror the glory of the Lord, are constantly being transfigured into His very own image in ever increasing splendor and from one degree of glory to another; [for this comes] from the Lord [Who is] the Spirit."*

The key word here is *continued.*

Without interruption, or distraction, we need to face the mirror of God's Word and allow it to transform us.

Consider a mirror. It always accurately reflects, or imitates, what is put before it. The problem is, if God's Word is a mirror, then this would explain why we feel so inferior at times. What we are reading in His Word, and what our lives actually *look* like, are often two totally different things.

But therein is also the solution! As we continue in God's Word, we are *"constantly being transfigured into His very own image in ever increasing splendor and from one degree of glory to another."* The mirror of God's Word isn't like the mirror in my bathroom. It has the unique ability to show me what *God* sees, not what I see.

To be transfigured, or transformed, describes something that happens from the inside out. **Christ is in us.** Therefore, with each decision we make to honor Him and His Word, He is revealed more and more through us. This is why the Bible says we are being changed into His image with ever increasing glory!

But notice this transformation takes place one decision at a time. In other words, every time I make a decision for righteousness, I shine brighter and brighter reflecting Him more and more. And this doesn't just apply to what I believe about myself. Righteousness describes the new person—spirit, soul, and body.

The Bible says, *"You've become a new person. This new person is continually renewed in knowledge to be like its Creator. Where this happens, there is no Greek or Jew, circumcised or uncircumcised, barbarian, uncivilized person, slave or free person. Christ is everything and in everything" (Colossians 3:10-11).*[1] In other words, it doesn't matter where you came from or what you've done, once you've accepted Christ, you are new on the inside. And eventually, that "new" should show up on the outside.

For example, my decision to choose love, have patience, forgive others and myself, submit to authority, honor people, and be willing and ready to give to those in need despite my own needs, will reflect Christ in me.

Here's what the writer of Colossians went on to say:

"As holy people whom God has chosen and loved, be sympathetic, kind, humble, gentle, and patient. Put up with each other, and forgive each other if anyone has a complaint. Forgive as the Lord forgave you. Above all, be loving. This ties everything together perfectly. Also, let Christ's perfect peace control you. God has called you into this peace by bringing you into one body. Be thankful. Let Christ's word with all its wisdom and richness live in you. Use psalms, hymns, and spiritual songs to teach and instruct yourselves about God's kindness. Sing to God in your hearts. Everything you say or do should be done in the name of the Lord Jesus, giving thanks to God the Father through Him" (3:12-17).[2]

Can I just remind you these instructions apply to your

The face is the mirror of the mind, and eyes without speaking confess the secrets of the heart.

-St. Jerome

mirror first? **Before you can ever truly reflect Christ toward others, you must first see Christ in you.**

- Be kind, humble, gentle, and patient with yourself.

- Forgive yourself as the Lord has forgiven you.

- Love yourself, and let His peace control you.

- Be thankful and let God reveal His kindness to you.

As Christians, we know these should be our actions toward others, but what does it say about God's Word when we withhold these same actions toward ourselves?

Mirror, Mirror, on the Wall
Who is really Lord of all?
Mirror, Mirror, on the Wall
Christ in me means hope for all!

Vessels of Honor

In my house, I have a beautiful vase in my entryway. It is set there to warmly greet my guests. We could say it is a

vessel of honor. But in my kitchen, I have a trashcan—
another vessel, but not as honorable. Both are in my
house by my choice, and both serve a purpose. But in the
real world, my trashcan can never decide it wants to be a
vase. Its fate is sealed and it will forever be a trashcan.

Did you know this is not so in the house of God?

The Apostle Paul said, *"In a great house there are not only
vessels of gold and silver, but also of wood and clay, some
for honor and some for dishonor. Therefore if anyone
cleanses himself from the latter, he will be a vessel for
honor, sanctified and useful for the Master, prepared for
every good work" (2 Timothy 2:20-21).* The great house
he speaks of is a depiction of God's house. In it, God has
many types of vessels (describing those who have been
welcomed in through faith in Christ).

But notice Paul said some vessels are for honor and
some for dishonor. A better translation is *"...some for
honorable and noble [use] and some for menial and
ignoble [use]."* [3] The word *ignoble* describes something of
low character, or low grade or quality, something
inferior. This is often how we feel about ourselves when

we come to Christ, and according to this scripture, if we don't make the necessary changes it is how we'll remain.

But unlike my trashcan, who is forever doomed to remain as such, you and I have a choice. *"If anyone cleanses himself from the latter* [from being a vessel of dishonor], *he will be a vessel for honor, sanctified and useful for the Master, prepared for every good work."* In other words, when you and I make conscious decisions to reflect Christ by allowing Him to work in our heart, we are transformed into a vessel of honor!

I can attest to this truth. When I became a Christian, I was a lot like the trashcan—full of negativity, judgments, and fears. And none of these words describe our righteousness in Christ. Little by little however, I made adjustments to my behavior (acting from the inside out) by allowing God's Word to change me. One decision at a time, I was transformed more and more into His image.

Have I arrived yet? No, of course not. But accepting His love and forgiveness of my sins, and then in turn, forgiving myself and accepting who He has made me to be, in addition to righteous decisions for good and not evil, I am now a vessel that shines brighter and brighter for my Savior.

What's Your Value?

The real clincher to my transformation however, was when I realized God saw me with value whether I was like the trashcan or the vase.

Let me ask this question: If I offered you a $100 bill, would you take it? Of course you would. Why? Because it has value. But what if I took that same $100 bill and wadded it up, threw it down, stepped on it, ground it into the dirt to the point it had minor tears in it, would you still take it?

Yes! Because regardless of its condition, it still has value.

And this is true of you and I in the eyes of God. No matter our condition, He sees us with value. He sees our potential, and better than that, He sees Christ in us! And this fact alone makes us of infinite worth to God.

This is why the Bible says the reflection of a believer in their mirror reflects the glory of the Lord. It is Christ in you. *"But we all, with unveiled face, **beholding as in a*** *mirror the glory of the Lord, are being transformed into the same image from glory to glory, just as by the Spirit of the Lord" (2 Corinthians 3:18).*

From glory to glory, from faith to faith, from one revelation to another, God transforms us into His image by His Spirit. Our value is not lost based on performance. Our usefulness might be, but never our value.

What do I mean by that?

It would be silly for me to put roses in my trashcan and set it out in my entryway to greet guests. In the same way, God recognizes how we reflect Him draws others to Him or pushes them away. If God had made me a national speaker when I was a young Christian, I would've been a horrible representative! I had a potty-mouth, I was a complainer, I was ignorant of God's love, barely being able to accept it for myself, and so on.

But from one degree of glory to another, He has changed me into a vessel that reflects Him more accurately.

What Do You See?

I read a story about a man whose grandmother would

position him in front of the mirror when he was a child. She would stand there degrading him, telling him what she thought about him. As a result, he grew up to *hate* mirrors. He avoided them at all cost. They were only a reminder of the pain inflicted on him as a child.

As irony would have it, when his grandmother died, he received her antique mirror as a part of her last will and testament. This infuriated him and he considered throwing it away, but decided instead to put it in the attic as a form of imprisonment for the awful mirror.

This man never came to terms with his reflection. He was unable to see the glory of the Lord (God's potential within him) reflecting back. Instead, his reflection only duplicated the bitterness of his own soul. Mirrors give faithful views of its counterpart. When you stand before a mirror and wave, it waves. When you smile, it smiles. If you are bitter, it is bitter. If you feel inferior to it, it feels inferior to you.

But...

If you see Christ in your mirror, it will reflect Christ back to you. If you see hope, love, and acceptance, your mirror will reflect back to you what you see.

"So all of us who have had that veil removed can see and reflect the glory of the Lord. And the Lord—who is the Spirit—makes us more and more like Him as we are changed into His glorious image" (2 Corinthians 3:18).[4]

Chapter Fourteen

Awakening

A single event can awaken a stranger within us totally unknown to us. To live is to be slowly born.
-Antoine de Saint-Exupery

In 1969, a doctor went to work at a facility which dealt with patients who had long-term (if not life-long) chronic and extremely debilitating diseases. This particular doctor was assigned to victims of an encephalitis epidemic, which left them in a catatonic state. Once vibrant, they were now no longer able to do anything for themselves. With their arms and hands in crimped positions, they simply gazed in midair all day. And when spoken to, they were unable to respond. However, quite by accident, the doctor discovered one of his patients had a surprising reflex. When he threw a baseball towards her from across the room, her crimped arm would reach out spontaneously and catch the ball although she continued to appear otherwise non-responsive.

To make a long story short, the doctor began performing a variety of tests on his patients to find out if they were awake on the inside although they appeared catatonic on the outside. That summer, the doctor administered doses of an experimental drug to all his patients, and miraculously, they all *awakened*. Some of them had been in a semi-unconscious condition for 25-30 years, but now they were talking, walking, and interacting with others. It was truly amazing.

But unfortunately, their "awakening" didn't last. The medicine had only a short-term effect on the patients and after a few months they all returned to their lifeless state for no known reason. In the end, the doctor determined that although he had no understanding as to what helped or didn't help, he knew one thing for sure: **Every human being has an inner person which needs to be awakened regardless of what we can see on the outside.**[1]

Is this not true of our spiritual lives? Paul once said, *"Awake to Righteousness...!" (1 Corinthians 15:34)*.

Before receiving Christ and salvation, all human beings

are physically alive, yet spiritually catatonic. However, when the Spirit of the Living God makes His home within the heart of a believer, there is a great awakening. *"If any man be in Christ, he is a new creation..." (2 Corinthians 5:17).* Physically, we may look the same on the day of our salvation as we did the day before, but we are not the same. And over time, that which has come alive on the inside begins to show itself on the outside.

I am not the same person today that I was before being born-again. In fact, if I ever tell stories of my past, most people have a hard time believing me because it describes a person who is much different than who I am now.

An anonymous author once wrote, **"If every day is an awakening, you will never grow old. You will just keep growing."** This is how it is with our salvation. When our spirit man is born-again (awakened to new life), every day becomes an opportunity to grow in Christ. Every day can be an awakening. For example, when God set me in front of my mirror and said, *"Now you tell her you love her and you forgive her,"* a darkened area of my heart was awakened to truth.

I believe this principle is some of the underlying meaning to Paul's words to the church in Rome when he said, *"And do this, knowing what [a critical] hour this is, how it is high time now for you to wake up out of your sleep (rouse to reality). For salvation (final deliverance) is nearer to us now than when we first believed (adhered to, trusted in, and relied on Christ, the Messiah)" (Romans 13:11).[2]* He wasn't speaking of awaking from literal sleep. Paul was referring to the catatonic state we once walked in before Christ and the danger of falling back into a similar condition.

> *Every issue, belief, attitude, or assumption is precisely the issue that stands between you and your relationships; and between you and yourself.*
>
> -Author Unknown

Salvation is not a one-time event in a person's life. It may have begun on a certain day, but it is journey. Salvation is deliverance, safety, preservation, healing and soundness of mind. Each of us need these provisions on a daily basis, not just one time at its introduction.

This is why it is so very important for us to awake to righteousness! As you've been learning in this book, righteousness is both a position and an action. It is first our right-standing with God, including our ability to stand before Him without guilt or inferiority as if we had never sinned –and then righteousness is our response to God's grace. It is the daily fruit we bear in our lives as we *"...do everything in word or deed in the name of the Lord Jesus, giving thanks to God the Father through Him"* *(Colossians 3:17).*

Jesus said, *"Let your light so shine before men, that they may see your good works and glorify your Father in heaven" (Matthew 5:16).* We are living in a critical hour. We don't know when our Savior will return for His Church, we only know it is one day closer today than it was yesterday. It *"...is nearer to us now than when we first believed..."* The scriptures encourage us to awake (and stay awake) to righteousness because *"In the way of righteousness is life, and in its pathway there is no death"* *(Proverbs 12:28).*

Carl Gustav Jung said, "Your vision will become clear only when you look into your heart ... [he] who looks outside, dreams. [He] who looks inside, awakens."

It is Christ within us! The very thought of it should cause our hearts to leap with inexpressible joy. An understanding of righteousness should be our motivation everyday to remain awake in the midst of a dark world. Jesus gave us this warning: *"Are there not twelve hours in the day? Anyone who walks about in the daytime does not stumble, because he sees [by] the light of this world. But if anyone walks about in the night, he stumbles, because there is no light in him [the light is lacking to him]" (John 11:9-10).*[3]

We have been awakened by the True Light. Jesus is the *"...life, and His life [is] the light of men" (John 1:4).* The world around us is dark and we are often tempted to sleep instead of shining our light in the darkness. But we have been awakened and there is reason to rejoice.

How Fortunate We Are

The Message Bible says, *"What a God we have! And how fortunate we are to have Him, this Father of our Master Jesus! Because Jesus was raised from the dead, we've been given a brand-new life and have everything to live for, including a future in heaven—and the future starts now!*

God is keeping careful watch over us and the future. The Day is coming when you'll have it all —life healed and whole. I know how great this makes you feel, even though you have to put up with every kind of aggravation in the meantime. Pure gold put in the fire comes out of it proved pure; genuine faith put through this suffering comes out proved genuine. When Jesus wraps this all up, it's your faith, not your gold, that God will have on display as evidence of His victory. You never saw Him, yet you love Him. You still don't see Him, yet you trust Him —with laughter and singing. Because you kept on believing, you'll get what you're looking forward to: total salvation" (1 Peter 1:3-9).

How fortunate we are! Did you know the dictionary defines the word fortunate as lucky? I'm pretty confident the Apostle Peter wasn't referring to luck. "Lucky" describes something that happens by chance or by accident—not intentional. The patients in my earlier story did not awaken by luck. The doctor was intentionally trying to cure them. He was fortunate to have found something that worked—however brief it was.

In the same way, the life we have been given through salvation is anything but lucky! It was definitely intentional on God's part. This is why Peter rejoiced in saying, *"What a God we have!"*

We, who have received Jesus as our Lord and Savior, are most fortunate! Synonyms include blessed, encouraged, favored, happy, promising, rosy, triumphant, victorious, well-off, and well-to-do! Why are we blessed? Why are we encouraged and happy? Why are we favored, rosy, and triumphant? Because we have been given a brand-new life in Christ Jesus! And this life is now a life worth living!

And not only that, but it's never going to end. Eternal Life is a quality of life that started at salvation but never ends. We don't have to sing, "In the sweet by and by..." while we wait for this miserable life to end and heaven to receive (and rescue) us. NO! Eternity has been placed in our hearts by the power of the Living God who gave up His only begotten Son so that we may have life, and life more abundantly.

Is heaven going to be wonderful? You bet! We can only

imagine what it will truly be like. I have had some times with God where I am just swept away in the revelation of His goodness; times where I am literally overwhelmed with such joy that it feels like my heart might just bust. I think heaven will be like that... *and more.* No wonder those who have tasted heaven early chose to stay rather than return to earth. As the Apostle Paul said, *"For me, to live is Christ, and to die is gain" (Philippians 1:21).* There is a day coming when we will have it all. But for now, *"...to [truly] live is Christ..."* and for that we are most fortunate.

Remain Solid

My challenge to you now is this: Whatever you believe, believe it with all your heart. The biblical example of being double-minded like waves of the sea is so true of the inconsistent. One minute they seem strong in their conviction, but with a little peer pressure or persuasion, they flip and change like a pancake in a skillet. James said, *"People who 'worry their prayers' are like wind-whipped waves. Don't think you're going to get anything from the Master that way, adrift at sea, keeping all your options open" (James 1:6-8).*[4] Isn't that what we're doing when we aren't firm in our belief system? We're really just *"keeping all our options open..."*—just in case.

Just in case what? Just in case God isn't who He says He is? Just in case God's Word is a lie, and not the truth? Just in case it's more popular to be quiet about your faith and freedom in Christ? Or just in case it's politically correct to "go with the flow" letting others dictate your identity? What pleases God is your faith—*not your changing belief system.*

So I'm challenging you to decide:

Are you the righteousness of God in Christ, or not?

It's good to have a teachable spirit—humble before God, not pretending to know-it-all. But what do YOU believe? Are you solid in it? Or on the fence waiting for a strong wind to push you one way or the other? It'd be nice if you could guarantee the strong wind was a "strong" faith friend who'd push you in the right direction. But, in your ignorance and lack of decision, you might be pushed in the wrong direction by a *loud* friend (not necessarily a smart one). *"[And] that's why Jesus lived and died and then lived again: so that He could be our Master across the entire range of life and death, and free us from the petty tyrannies of each other" (Romans 14:9).*[5]

You Believe This Stuff!

As I travel and speak on the topic of righteousness, I am often introduced to new people and places. During a particular weekend retreat, my message of righteousness also took on a flair of faith and believing. Sometimes, its not enough to only teach on this subject. I often feel compelled to also challenge people to *believe* the message of righteousness because religion has made it out to seem pious, or unattainable.

After my third session, a precious elderly woman in her seventies approached me and said, "You know what makes you so good?" [Now pause for a second, and think about how you would answer that!] While I considered what she just said, she looked me square in the eyes and said, "Because *you* believe this stuff!" I laughed and responded, "Why yes ma'am, I do! And so should you!"

Sadly, she explained that she had listened to many teachers over the years, but didn't always think they believed God's Word. And I sympathized because at one time I didn't either. My feelings and the thoughts in my head were often in complete opposition to God's Word. And I dare say this is true of everyone.

But let's try looking at things through an eternal perspective. I remember hearing a story about a lady who was upset with her husband because he loved old western movies. She wanted him to get up and do something constructive instead of just sitting there in front of the TV. As she was folding clothes in the other room, fuming about how relaxed he was in his chair, the Holy Spirit said to her, *"And what does this have to do with eternity?"* The obvious answer was: not much.

There's a lesson there for us as well. Instead of getting all upset about what others believe, why don't we make sure we're solid in what we believe? *"Cultivate your own relationship with God, but don't impose it on others. You're fortunate if your behavior and your belief are coherent (harmonious). But if you're not sure, if you notice that you are acting in ways inconsistent with what you believe... then you know that you're out of line. And if the way you live isn't consistent with what you believe, then it's wrong" (Romans 14:22-23).*[6]

My point is, although you and I are guaranteed to have days where we struggle, make mistakes, and simply dislike ourselves, it doesn't change God's Word. He has declared us to be the righteousness of God in Him despite our shortcomings. The Bible says, *"The kingdom of God isn't about eating and drinking—it's [about] righteousness and peace and joy in the Holy Spirit. If you serve Christ with this attitude, you will please God, and others will approve of you too" (Romans 14:17-18).*[7]

Pleasing God with your faith starts with righteousness—your simple faith in Christ for the forgiveness of sins. Then it's a chain reaction from *righteousness* to *peace* to *joy*! **If you're lacking peace and joy, you can be sure there's a snag in your belief system regarding righteousness.**

It's normal for human beings to struggle with the balance between natural and spiritual principles. This is why God outlined His truth in His Word and then gave us the testimonies of others to encourage us along the way.

For example, the Apostle Paul had experiences with God that could not be explained in the natural, so he described it this way: *"I know a man in Christ who fourteen years ago—whether in the body I do not know, or whether out of the body I do not know, God knows—such a one was caught up to the third heaven. And I know such a man—whether in the body or out of the body I do not know, God knows—how he was caught up into Paradise and heard inexpressible words, which it is not lawful for a man to utter.* **Of such a one I will boast***..."* (2 Corinthians 12:2-5).

Who was this man he was referring to? Theologians all agree it was himself. Paul was referring to who he was in Christ. In an endeavor to describe his experiences with God, he was so caught up in the *revelation* of who God is and who we are in Him, that he wasn't even sure if it was an in- or out-of-body experience. He just knew it wasn't him, *the mortal man*; it was him, *the man in Christ*.

But there is a natural side too. Peter rejoiced over how fortunate we are to be saved, yet he said, *"I know how great this makes you feel, even though you have to put up with every kind of aggravation in the meantime."* How true is that? No matter how much I learn about this life in Christ, and the righteousness we have received through Him, there are still days I am tempted to pull my hair out. But obviously I don't because of what I have learned about our life in Christ. As Peter explained, *"Pure gold put in the fire comes out proved pure; genuine faith put through this suffering [this occasional aggravation] comes out proved genuine."* Why? Because in all things we have the victory in Christ Jesus. There really is nothing to lose; only everything to gain!

Let me repeat Paul's admonishment to us: *"For me, to live is Christ, and to die is gain!"* Sounds like a win-win situation to me... how about to you?

Do you believe this way?

Are you convinced yet?

If you love Jesus, your answer should be yes. It's true you may still be growing in this revelation. But the Holy Spirit is always ready to reveal these truths to you. Think about it, *"You never saw Him, yet you love Him. You still don't see Him, yet you trust Him..."* Don't you think there's more to the package (this life in Christ) than what you know right now? It doesn't matter who we are, or where we are, in our walk with God. As Christians, there is always more to learn, more to be revealed, and more to experience! How fortunate we really are!

And the goal is to keep on believing! Sure, *"...for a little while [now], you have been grieved by various trials..." (1 Peter 1:6),* but that isn't cause to quit believing. On the contrary, it is all the more reason to *keep* believing. Lean on God's faithfulness. Remember, *"If we are faithless, He remains faithful; He cannot deny Himself" (2 Timothy 2:13).* And the result of your continued faith in God? Total salvation! The word total means whole, entire, full-blown, full-scale, undisputed, unlimited, and thorough!

This is your salvation. This is the life we now live in Christ, and the fullness of it is still being revealed.

How fortunate (blessed, encouraged, favored, happy, promising, rosy, triumphant, victorious, well-off, and well-to-do) you and I are as the righteousness of God in Christ!

Chapter Fifteen

Living Out Our Righteousness

A little knowledge that acts is worth infinitely more than much knowledge that is idle.
-Kahill Gibran

People have asked me, "Daphne, why do you talk so much about righteousness?"

For starters, the word righteousness is mentioned 292 times in the New King James Bible alone. This makes me think it might be important to God. And secondly, my understanding of it has been so much more than mere knowledge. I now have a *faith* I live by, a *purpose* I live for, and (thanks to the message of righteousness) a *self* I can live with.

But I don't want to keep it to myself any more than the Apostle Paul wanted to keep his revelation to himself. In fact in Philippians 3:1, he said, *"My brethren, rejoice in the Lord. For me to write the same things to you is not tedious, but for you it is safe."* Other translations read, *"I never tire of telling you these things; I do it to safeguard*

191

your faith." [1] *"It's no trouble for me to write [or tell] you the same things over and over. It will help you be more ready [for whatever comes your way]."* [2] And this is my primary reason also.

I'm not sure how many *Switchfoot* fans I have reading this book, but my children introduced me to their music and although their style is a little harder than my softer side, they have become a favorite because of the lyrics of a particular song entitled, Mess of Me.[3] It goes like this:

> *I am my own affliction*
> *I am my own disease*
> *There ain't no drug that they could sell*
> *There ain't no drug to make me well*
>
> *Because the sickness is myself*
> *I made a mess of me*
> *I wanna get back the rest of me*
> *I made a mess of me*
> *But I wanna spend the rest of my life alive*
>
> *We lock our souls in cages*
> *We hide inside our shells*
> *And it's hard to free the ones you love*
> *When you can't forgive yourself*

The truth these lyrics speak of are just another reason I keep spreading the good news of God's righteousness to this generation. I have come to realize: **A faith to live by and a purpose to live for are of no matter if you don't have a SELF you can live with.**

You are not the affliction. You are not the disease. Jesus came to change all that. *"For He made Him who knew no sin to be sin for YOU, that YOU might become the righteousness of God in Him" (2 Corinthians 5:21).*

Step One

Throughout this book, I've repeatedly shared with you how the Holy Spirit prompted me to *say* something. I was slow to realize the power of my own voice. The objective of the Holy Spirit was to teach me how to see myself differently by changing the way I think. Through my own confession—*saying* aloud what God had already said of me in His Word—my self-image began to change in proportion to what I was saying.

It wasn't enough to simply know: *"There's no condemnation for those who are in Christ Jesus"* or *"I'm the righteousness of God in Christ."* I was only able to embrace these truths because the Holy Spirit had me continually confess them.

2 Corinthians 4:13 states: *"And since we have the same spirit of faith, according to what is written, 'I believed and therefore I spoke,' we also believe and therefore speak."* **It is very important for you to speak your faith**. You won't always feel forgiven or righteous (much less worthy of such), but regardless, you must learn to confess God's Word in faith, believing it is true. This is step one.

Hebrews 11:1-3 says, *"Faith is the substance of things hoped for, the evidence of things not seen. For by it the elders obtained a good testimony. By faith we understand that the worlds were framed by the word of God, so that the things which are seen were not made of things which are visible."* In other words, the world was created by the "word" of God. We know in Genesis God "spoke" and "it was," so although God's word was not "seen," it was *creative* in power.

As children of God, we have been given the same ability. This is why the writer of Hebrews said, *"...by [faith] the elders obtained a good testimony…"* referring to the prophets (those who came before Christ). They had a spirit of faith, and *we* have the *same spirit of faith*.

By biblical definition, *"Faith is the substance of things hoped for, the evidence of things not seen"*—whereas a "spirit" of faith describes what we are doing with what we believe. The Apostle Paul said, *"…I believe and therefore I speak…"*

The problem is most of us haven't understood the power of speaking our faith. We were taught that to have faith you must believe in Christ; but we've forgotten we had to *confess* Him also. **How we *began* in faith is how we must *continue* in faith—through our believing and speaking.**

But since this is foreign to most of us who have always had a quiet faith, we have to be trained. And this is exactly what the Holy Spirit did in my life. I didn't always believe the confessions He was having me make, but the Holy Spirit knew my spirit would be transformed nonetheless. And thankfully, we have the disciples of Jesus as another example of this. They too, had to be "schooled" into a spirit of faith.

Faith School

We find our lesson in Mark 11:22-23, when Jesus explained to His disciples how to operate in faith. After passing by a fig tree Jesus had cursed the day before, the disciples saw it had withered up and were amazed, so they questioned Him about it. Mark Hankins says, "Jesus could have told His disciples, 'Now this is a Deity trick that only Me, God, and the Holy Spirit know how to do, so don't try this at home.'"

But that's *not* what Jesus said...

On the contrary, He told them, *"Have faith in God" (Mark 11:22).* If, by this statement, Jesus meant for us to only believe God, His following words would've been something like: *"God is faithful and trustworthy, therefore have faith in Him."* But instead, Jesus continued by telling His disciples (and us) HOW to have faith. In other words, Jesus was really telling them, *"Have the God-kind of faith."*

What is the God-kind of faith? Well, for starters, God

spoke and it was. Doing the same, Jesus spoke to the fig tree and it changed. Even Abraham changed his circumstances through his confession.

For example, Paul said Abraham exercised the God-kind of faith when, *"...contrary to* [natural] *hope in* [spiritual] *hope he believed, so that he became the father of many nations according to what was spoken..." (Romans 4:18).* In other words, despite how he felt or what it looked like, Abraham said what God said. He called himself the father of many nations as if he had many descendents although he did not yet have any children. He declared what was going to be, not necessarily what *was* at the moment.

This is why Paul said, *"And since we have the same spirit of faith, according to what is written, 'I believed and therefore I spoke,' we also believe and therefore speak."* Faith is BELIEVING and SPEAKING. It's not enough for you and I to just *believe.*

Jesus said, *"For assuredly, I tell you, whoever SAYS to this mountain, 'Be removed and be cast into the sea,' and does not doubt in his heart, but **believes** that those things he*

SAYS will be done, he will have whatever he SAYS" (Mark 11:23).

Did you notice the emphasis Jesus put on what we say? He mentioned *saying* three times and *believing* only once. This is why you and I can "school" ourselves into faith. The formula Jesus gave us is 3:1. For every three times you speak your faith, your believing will increase by one.

But most of the time, when people are in a pressure situation, they zip their lips and say nothing because Momma always said, "If you can't say something nice, don't say anything at all!" But Momma's instructions weren't meant to be applied to speaking our faith—in that case, we need to do just the opposite.

So our formula is: **3 parts say = 1 part belief**

FAITH is believing and speaking. Therefore, to increase your believing (or your faith), YOU MUST SPEAK.

Revelation

As I was learning and meditating on this myself, the Holy Spirit showed me an example of a post office. In Romans

10:17, the Bible says, *"Faith comes by hearing, and hearing by the Word."* And we've already read, *"Faith is the substance of things hoped for..."* (Hebrews 11:1).

When I lived out in the country, my mail and packages had to be picked up at our local Post Office. So the Holy Spirit said to me: *"Hearing the Word of God is an example of how faith COMES [just like your packages that arrive at the post office]. But faith is RECEIVED when you actually take them home and open them."*

In other words, people can get to a place where they are receiving what they need (such as letters of promise and packages of inheritance) as they study and get revelation of God's Word. But then just like the person who tossed a letter on the table, not realizing it contained something valuable, we too can leave our promises *unopened*, never fully receiving what God has given to us. But, on the other hand, *opening* our mouth and speaking aloud what God has said of us in His Word is how we unseal His promises for ourselves. And if we are struggling with believing God's promises, it is also how we "school" ourselves into faith.

Webster's defines faith as: a firm belief in something for
which there is no proof.[4]

This is a good definition, but it also explains why people
are weak in faith. If faith is a firm belief or persuasion,
and a person is not yet firmly persuaded, then what?
Then we need to go back to Jesus' instruction in Mark
11:23 and do a whole lot more *saying*! Remember our
formula is:

3 parts say = 1 part belief

This is why the Word of God in your mouth is so
powerful, while the Word of God on your shelf isn't. Until
someone speaks it, it just lies dormant.

Locate Your Faith

Another word we need to understand is *perception*.
Webster's defines it as: to become aware of through the
senses, and especially through sight.[5] This is where
people get snagged. We are guilty of building our faith
on our senses or sight instead of by what God has said in
His Word.

Up until now, I dare say you have predominantly lived by

perception (or your senses). All of us have! We learned at an early age to live by what we see, feel, hear, and smell. This isn't entirely wrong, but it's not how you operate in a spirit of faith. The Bible says, *"For we walk by faith, not by sight" (2 Corinthians 5:7).* Yet most do just the opposite—which might explain why the enemy has been able to take such advantage of us.

So remember this: faith is the substance of things hoped for, the evidence of things not seen. There are two parts to our faith:

- <u>Part One is believing</u>: it is the *substance*, or raw material, we give God to work with.
- <u>Part Two is speaking</u>: it is the *evidence* of things not seen. These are our words.

Words can be heard but not seen. This is why if you and I spent a little time together, I would know fairly quickly where your faith is simply by listening to you. Matthew 12:34 says, *"Out of the abundance of the heart the mouth speaks."*

If you want to grow in faith and walk in the promises of God, YOU MUST HAVE BOTH PARTS. Even if you start with *zero* believing, you can build faith by *speaking*. Never in the Word of God does it say, "If you just believe, and say nothing, you'll have what you believe."

Faith in Action

Let me give you an example of faith in action. Hebrews, Chapter 11 is known as the "Faith Hall of Fame." It is a record of men and women who activated their faith, received their promises, and pleased God in the process. For the sake of example, I'm going to replace the word "faith" in a few of these passages with the words "believing and speaking" to illustrate how a *spirit* of faith works.

"By [believing and speaking], *Abel obtained a good testimony" (verse 4). "By* [believing and speaking], *Enoch [pleased God] (verse 5). "By* [believing and speaking], *Abraham obeyed when he was called to go out..." (verse 8). "By* [believing and speaking], *Sarah herself received strength to conceive..." (verse 11). "By* [believing and speaking], *Moses forsook Egypt, not fearing the wrath of the king; for he endured as seeing Him who is invisible" (verse 27). "By* [believing and speaking], *the harlot Rahab*

did not perish with those who did not believe, when she had received the spies with peace."

Pause for a moment.

This is the FAITH HALL OF FAME. Did the scriptures have to call Rahab a *harlot*? Couldn't it have simply said she was a woman who pleased God when she helped the spies? No, because at the time she was a harlot, yet in God's eyes, **her past was not an indicator of her future.** And the same is true for you and I! In other words, by faith (by believing and speaking) our current situation can change.

Never get caught up in labels. Jesus said we would have what *we* say, not what others say.[6]

Hebrews 11:32-34 continues: *"And what more shall I say? For the time would fail me to tell of Gideon and Barak and Samson and Jephthah, also of who through faith* [believing and speaking] *subdued kingdoms, worked righteousness, obtained promises, stopped the mouths of lions, quenched the violence of fire, escaped the edge of the sword, out of weakness were made strong, became valiant in battle, and turned to flight the armies of their enemies!"*

These men and women did amazing feats through faith. But don't forget it wasn't by believing only—they also spoke what they believed, and God met them at their confession.

> *All the art of living lies in a fine mingling of letting go and holding on.*
> -Havelock Ellis

So What Now?

As a believer in Christ, you have been declared righteous and acceptable before God. You have been given the ability to stand before Him without guilt or inferiority as if you had never sinned. It is not something you are working towards. This gift was given to you when you were born-again.

And I know you've blown it more than once since the day of salvation—so have I. So what now? Just because you have begun to understand who you are in Christ and that your performance is not getting you any closer to righteousness than you already were, do you now have the freedom to do whatever you want? No. Sin is sin and it's nothing to laugh at or take lightly. But, because we can all fall into sin at one time or another, we need to remember its effect.

A minister once said 1 John 1:9 is the Christian's "bar of soap," which says, *"If we confess our sins, He is faithful and just to forgive us our sins and to cleanse us from all unrighteousness."* So let me ask you a question: If all the unrighteousness is cleansed when we confess our sins, what is left? *Righteousness.*

On the first day of salvation, you prayed and accepted Jesus as your Lord and Savior. You were then cleansed, given a clean slate and declared righteous before God. So, now also, when you confess your sins to God, you can lift your head from prayer just as you did on the very first day and accept your right-standing with Him. For He said in Isaiah 43:25, *"I—yes, I alone—am the one who blots out your sins for My own sake and will never think of them again."* He is not keeping a record of your forgiven sins (and neither should you).

And remember, *"There is therefore now no condemnation for those who are in Christ Jesus" (Romans 8:1).* This very minute, if you slip up and blow it, you can immediately *(right now)* ask for forgiveness and move forward without guilt or condemnation. Every day is a new day and every minute is a new minute. When you confess and repent, God forgives and forgets and puts you back in right-standing with Himself. You are re-established in righteousness.

But it doesn't end there. You will have to *pursue* these things because the devil wants to rob us of our knowledge of who we are in Christ and the blessings we've freely received. First Timothy 6:11-12 says, *"But you, O man of God, flee [immoral] things and **pursue righteousness**, godliness, faith, love, patience, gentleness. Fight the good fight of faith, lay hold on eternal life, to which you were also called and have confessed the good confession in the presence of many witnesses."*

You must pursue righteousness. You can't earn it—but you can *guard* and *protect* it by setting your mind on the things of God and not the things of your flesh. But be prepared, it is a fight. You still have a flesh nature that wants to contradict what you now know to be true. You must fight the good *"fight of faith"* because your feelings will always try to dictate your faith (and it's a fight)!

But Paul also said to *"lay hold on eternal life."* It's not enough to know you will live forever in Heaven with God. You must lay hold, grasp, take for yourself the eternal life—and quality of life—Jesus purchased for you. This is only accomplished by renewing your mind daily in God's Word. Jeremiah 29:11 says God has a plan for every believer. *"For I know the thoughts that I think toward you, says the Lord, thoughts of peace and not of evil, to give you a future and a hope."* But we are responsible for getting into His Word and finding out for ourselves what those thoughts and plans are. The devil would like nothing more than to block or water down our understanding of righteousness.

Deep Roots are Strong

The Bible has scripture after scripture referring to the "righteous" and every one of them is talking about those who have put their faith in Christ. For example, Psalm 92:12 says, *"The righteous shall flourish like a palm tree."* Have you ever noticed how palm trees are the only things still standing after a hurricane has ripped through a city?

It is because they have strong, deep roots. But unlike the deep roots of condemnation, which make us feel separated from God, the Bible says the righteous, referring to you and I, will *flourish* like the palm tree. In other words, when you push down deep and establish your roots in the knowledge of who you are in Christ, the devil will never win—no matter how hard a storm he blows your way.

Satan would love to keep you feeling insecure by making you think God has abandoned you in the storm, but don't believe it. Instead, put your faith in God's promises and hold on! Believe God's Word and keep speaking it!

> *Those who danced were thought to be quite insane by those who could not hear the music.*
> -Angela Monet

Act on Your Knowledge

But that's not all. Knowledge isn't enough if you don't act on it. *"But be doers of the word and not hearers only, deceiving yourselves. For if anyone is a hearer of the Word and not a doer, he is like a man observing his natural face in a mirror; for he observes himself, goes away, and immediately forgets what kind of man he was" (James 1:22-24).*

**Take a closer look into the perfect law of liberty—
*God's Word.*** Let it be your mirror.

*"He who looks into the perfect law of liberty and continues
in it, and is not a forgetful hearer but a doer of the work,
this one will be blessed in what he does" (James 1:25).*

I still blow it at times and it's tempting to stay
disappointed in myself. But I refuse to let guilt and
condemnation rule my life anymore—and neither should
you. Whether your feelings match what you know or not,
determine to believe God's Word and act on it. Then
hold your head high with the revelation He has forgiven
you and therefore your righteousness is intact.

Exercise Your Faith

Going back to speaking our faith, Mark Brazee has a
wonderful illustration on this subject. He says, "Faith is
like a muscle. Think back on a time when you physically
exerted yourself, such as in yard work or exercise, and
you found a muscle you hadn't used for awhile. Maybe it
hurt for two or three days, having become weak from
lack of use. If you start using that forgotten muscle

every day, it will actually grow in size and strength.

"However, if you let it lie dormant, then the next time you use it, you'll have to pump it up and get it working all over again. In the same manner, our capacity to operate in faith comes from hearing the Word of God, but our faith doesn't grow because we hear. We can feed and feed and feed a muscle, but it only grows in strength as we exercise it. Faith is the same way." [7]

You can use your faith (through your confession) to push insecurities and doubts away just like a weight lifter uses weights. Every time he pushes the weights away, he gains a little more strength. In the same way, every time you push the lies of the enemy away, you grow stronger.

Don't Lose What You've Gained

Jesus said in John 10:10, *"The thief does not come except to steal, and to kill, and to destroy. I have come that they may have life, and that they may have it more abundantly."* Remember, the devil's main purpose in this world is to *kill* your enthusiasm, *steal* your joy, and *destroy* your purpose.

In order to fight off the enemy and his plan to rob you from the freedom you have in Christ, you must never pick up the old dead man of sin and condemnation again. If you're not careful, you will naturally pick up old habits and lose what you've gained.

For example, when I was pregnant with our second child, Christopher, he was breach; and after months of waiting for him to turn, the doctors decided to turn him for me so I could have a natural delivery and avoid a c-section. I was told that as soon as they turned him in my womb, they would immediately begin to induce delivery. The doctors explained that if they allowed me to go home and wait for my body to begin labor on its own, the baby would flip back around to his original position because, *although it was dangerous*, it was what he was accustomed to and where he was comfortable.

In the same way, if you don't act on the truths you've learned in this book and begin to renew your mind to them immediately, you will naturally "flip back" to your original position, even though it was bondage (and dangerous).

Press Toward the Goal

It's now time to live out your righteousness! *You are the righteousness of God in Christ Jesus!* So face your mirror without condemnation. Pursue righteousness. Make a choice to serve God and not the flesh. Fight the good fight. And always press toward the goal.

As Paul summarized his understanding of who he was in Christ, let this be your confession also:

> *"[May I] be found in Him, not having my own righteousness, which is from the law, but that which is through faith in Christ, the righteousness which is from God by faith; that I may know Him and the power of His resurrection...[knowing that] I am still not all I should be, but I am focusing all my energies on this one thing: Forgetting the past and looking forward to what lies ahead, I strain to reach the end of the race and receive the prize for which God, through Christ Jesus, is calling us up to Heaven."* [8]

The Delay's

[top row] Christopher, Tya, Benjamin
[bottom] Daphne, Tod, Emily

Notes

Chapter One

1. New Living Translation
2. Rhema Bible Training Center | www.rhema.org
3. Philippians 4:7, New King James Version

Chapter Two

1. Genesis 1:26, New King James Version

Chapter Three

1. San Souci, Robert D. <u>Mulan</u>. [Video] Prod. Walt Disney Pictures, 1998.
2. Jones, Beth. <u>Getting a Grip on the Basics</u>. Harrison House, Inc., 1994.
3. Proverbs 23:7a, New King James Version
4. Spurgeon, Charles. The Fainting Warrior. [Sermon #235] Available at: http://www.spurgeon.org/sermons/ 0235.htm (accessed November 13, 2012).

Chapter Four

1. Where Grace Abounds | www.wheregraceabounds.org

Chapter Five

---

1. Carroll, Lewis. <u>Alice in Wonderland</u>. [Video] Prod. Walt Disney Pictures, 1951.
2. New Living Translation
3. New Living Translation
4. The Message Translation
5. New Living Translation
6. The Amplified Bible

Chapter Six

---

2. Burlingame, Michael. <u>For the People</u>. Available at: http://www.abrahamlincolnassociation.org/Newsletters/1-1.pdf (accessed November 13, 2012).
3. Genesis 2:17, New King James Version
4. New Living Translation
5. Leviticus 17:11, New Living Translation
6. New Living Translation
7. John 14:6, New King James Version

Chapter Seven

---

1. The Amplified Bible
2. New Living Translation
3. Webster's Encyclopedia Unabridged Dictionary of the English Language, s.v. *favor*.
4. New Living Translation

5. New Living Translation

6. GOD'S WORD Translation

7. Oldenburg, Ann. <u>$7M Car Giveaway Stuns TV Audience</u>. Available at: http://usatoday30.usatoday.com/life/people/2004-09-13-oprah-cars_x.htm (accessed November 13, 2012).

8. New Living Translation

Chapter Eight

1. New Living Translation

2. Vine's Expository Dictionary of New Testament Words, s.v. *justification*.

Chapter Nine

1. Daniel 6, New King James Version

2. New Living Translation

3. Kenyon, E.W. <u>New Creation Realities</u>. Kenyon's Gospel Publishing Society, Inc., 2000.

4. New Living Translation

5. New Living Translation

Chapter Eleven

1. New Living Translation

2. New Living Translation

Chapter Twelve

---

1. New Living Translation
2. The Amplified Bible

Chapter Thirteen

---

1. GOD'S WORD Translation
2. GOD'S WORD Translation
3. The Amplified Bible
4. GOD'S WORD Translation

Chapter Fourteen

---

1. http://www.oliversacks.com/about-the-author/biography (accessed November 13, 2012).
2. The Amplified Bible
3. The Amplified Bible
4. The Message Translation
5. The Message Translation
6. The Message Translation
7. New Living Translation

Chapter Fifteen

---

1. New Living Translation
2. New Century Version
3. Switchfoot. Mess of Me. [Album: Hello Hurricane]. 2009.

4. Webster's Encyclopedia Unabridged Dictionary of the English Language, s.v. *faith*.

5. Webster's Encyclopedia Unabridged Dictionary of the English Language, s.v. *perception*.

6. Mark 11:23, New King James Version

7. Brazee, Mark. <u>365 Days of Healing</u>. Harrison House, 1999, 2003, 2006.

8. Philippians 3:9-10, New King James Version; 3:13-14, New Living Translation

Daphne is a firm believer in application.
The companion workbook for *Facing the Mirror* is designed to help readers look into their own heart and belief system in order to apply these truths for themselves.

This workbook is ideal for individual or group study.

To order your copy, or to get more information, visit:

www.mirrorministries.org/products/facingthemirror

About the Author

Daphne Delay has been writing and speaking since 1999, when she was first asked to share at a women's conference. She wouldn't know at the time how profound that first speaking engagement would be. *But God knew...*

Daphne now travels and speaks frequently. She is the wife of a Senior Pastor and works side-by-side with her husband in the ministry at Family Harvest Church in Seminole, Texas. She is actively involved in their women's ministry and enjoys helping new believers build a foundation for a victorious life.

Daphne is an active "sports-mom." She loves attending all her kids' events. And besides writing, her second favorite hobby is anything to do with new technology. She doesn't mind being the "nerd" friend.

But what she wants to be remembered for most is:

Spreading the Good News of His Righteousness!

Contact Daphne

Updates and resources for *Facing the Mirror* can be found at:
mirrorministries.org/products/facingthemirror

For group or individual study, don't forget to get the
Workbook for *Facing the Mirror.*

Daphne speaks frequently on the topic of righteousness. She
can share a keynote, half-day, full-day, or retreat version of
this content, depending on your needs. If you are interested in
finding out more, please visit her Speaking page at:

mirrorministries.org/speaking

You can also connect with Daphne here:

Blog: *mirrorministries.org*

Twitter: *twitter.com/daphnedelay*

Facebook: *facebook.com/daphne.delay*